Discover God's Will

Five Factors That Will Change Your Life Forever

The Discover God Series

Thom O'Leary

www.DiscoverGodSeries.com

Creative Team Publishing
San Diego

Permissions and Credits in Order of Appearance:
- Scripture quotations marked (KJV) are taken from The Holy Bible, King James Version. Copyright 2000 by the Zondervan Corporation. All rights reserved.
- Scripture quotations marked (NIV) are taken from the Holy Bible, New International Version® NIV® Copyright © 1973, 1978, 1984, 2011 by Biblica, Inc.® Used by permission. All rights reserved worldwide.
- Scripture quotations marked (NLT) are taken from the Holy Bible. New Living Translation copyright© 1996, 2004, 2007 by Tyndale House Foundation. Used by permission of Tyndale House Publishers Inc., Carol Stream, Illinois 60188. All rights reserved.
- Scripture quotations marked (NKJV) are taken from the New King James Version®. Copyright © 1982 by Thomas Nelson, Inc. Used by permission. All rights reserved.
- Scripture taken from *The Message*. Copyright © 1993, 1994, 1995, 1996, 2000, 2001, 2002. Used by permission of NavPress Publishing Group.
- Quote from Sir Author Conan Doyle, author of *Sherlock Holmes* is used with permission of Andrea Plunket, Manager of the Sir Arthur Conan Doyle Estate.

- Erwin McManus Prays for His Son to be Dangerous: sermon illustration is used with permission from PreachingToday.com.
- Quarterback Tom Brady Still Searching: sermon illustration is used with permission from PreachingToday.com.

ISBN: 978-0-9884934-3-8
PUBLISHED BY CREATIVE TEAM PUBLISHING
www.CreativeTeamPublishing.com
San Diego

Printed in the United States of America

Endorsements on Behalf of

Discover God's Will

Five Factors That Will Change Your Life Forever

Steven Ford
Actor, Speaker
Son of President Gerald Ford

I have listened, learned, and enjoyed dozens and dozens of Thom's Sunday messages. This book will help you learn to hear God's voice for your life. It provides the tools to unfold God's roadmap for your journey.

*****

Chuck Fromm
Publisher and Founder of *Worship Leader* Magazine
25 years Pastor/President of Maranatha! Music

Discovering, living in and living out God's will is the lifetime walk of a true worshipper—a supernatural journey in Spirit and truth. Thom O'Leary offers a pastoral and in-depth roadmap to navigate what is one of the most challenging aspects of our relationship with God and others.

*****

Brock and Bodie Thoene
Best Selling Authors, *The Jerusalem Chronicles*

Pastor Thom O'Leary's book, *Discover God's Will—Five Factors That Will Change Your Life Forever* is essential reading for those who "love God and are called according to His purpose." The desire to know God's will... to discern with clarity and certainty that God is speaking to you personally... has existed throughout all ages and all cultures of the Church. Nevertheless, this present generation faces more NOISE—more challenges to hearing the "still, small voice"—than perhaps any before us. Noise: internal, external, electronic, social, and emotional.

Discover God's Will addresses that issue head on, with practical, easy to grasp steps. This volume will immediately become a favorite resource for personal use, for sharing with friends in need, and for teaching. It is anointed.

*****

Steve Potratz

Founder and President of The Parable Group

We serve a loving God who came that we might live life abundantly. There is no greater joy than discovering your unique you and then serving our Lord with the unique gifts He has given you. This book will lead you into the discovery of His good, pleasing and perfect will for your life. Thom has provided all of us a valuable resource and a fun read.

*****

Phil Strout

National Director of USA Vineyard Churches

Whenever I read a book I wonder if the author is echoing something that he or she might have heard, or is it something born from the school of reality and life. As I read through Thom's material I realized quickly that this was a voice, not an echo. "God's Will" is a big thing to tackle and I believe the reader will find some real help in this great adventure.

*****

Terrance Deal
Best Selling Author, *Leading With Soul*
Former Vanderbilt, USC, Stanford, and Harvard Professor

The secret to life is meaning, and people seek many pathways. One is the path directed by God evidenced in *Discover God's Will—Five Factors That Will Change Your Life Forever* by Thom O'Leary. Although Thom's path is different from mine, it is one that many will find encouraging and fruitful.

*****

Dana Nafziger
Former NFL Player
President and CEO of Aqua Systems, Inc.

Discover God's Will—Five Factors That Will Change Your Life Forever encourages us to take a closer look into our lives and acknowledge that we sometimes fall short of true peace and freedom in Christ. Revealed in these pages are some great scriptures and principles that will help us find God's perfect will for our lives. Having known Thom for quite some time, his loving, kind, gracious, and wise ways of presenting these Gospel truths are revealed in the fruit that we see in his life.

Discover God's Will

Five Factors That Will Change Your Life Forever

The Discover God Series

Thom O'Leary

www.DiscoverGodSeries.com

- The greatest discovery anyone can make is about who God is and what He wants for those who love and trust Him.

- You can discover God's will, God's purpose, and God's peace for your life.

- It's a lifelong journey that will change you forever.

Foreword

Kevin N. Springer
Pastor, Editor, and Writer
Co-Author, *Power Evangelism* with John Wimber

According to a recent Gallup poll, Americans attend church for two reasons: *"guidance* and spiritual growth" and "to keep grounded and *guided."*

No surprise there. From my experience as a pastor for more than 40 years, I concluded long ago that most people show up on Sundays to experience God and to know His will. That's why when my friend, Thom O'Leary asked me to write the Foreword to *Discover God's Will* I enthusiastically accepted.

Saint Augustine, the fourth-century Bishop of Hippo, discovered that if you wholeheartedly love God you will *want* to do what honors Him most. And that's why *Discover God's Will* is built on the premise that if you cultivate intimacy with Christ, His will flows to you and through you. God's love naturally flows in a supernatural way when we put Him first in everyday life.

Discover God's Will is spiritual and practical. It's a case built on five foundational, interlocking pillars (*factors*) that together direct us to "love God, and do what pleases Him."

The first pillar concerns the heart: Know Thyself—warts and all! Donald Grey Barnhouse once said, "I can say from experience that 95% of knowing the will of God consists in being prepared to do it before you know what it is." Being prepared begins with an honest inventory of the heart.

A prepared heart, an honest soul, hungers for God which is a part of the journey. We satiate that hunger, O'Leary notes, through knowing God's Word, communing with His people, cultivating an ear for His Spirit, and identifying with Christ through the pain of living in a broken, hostile world.

But none of this is of value unless we cultivate the disciplines of knowing God, and Thom O'Leary is perhaps at his best when talking about this pillar. This is where the rubber meets the road, the intersection of God touching souls, where we wait patiently and listen, and He speaks.

The fourth pillar, what for many is a fear factor, sobers us up, reminding us of our frailty and self-deception. Pastor Thom strikes hard at any tendency to morph loving God into loving self, or living in a thinly cloaked saccharine religiosity. Words and phrases like *submission, emotional health, serving others,* and *God's calling* remind us that knowing God's will can never be separated from loving God.

This leads to my favorite part of the book, the most personal and significant factor, which says that you cannot know God's will without passionately pursuing intimacy with Him through prayer and perseverance.

Knowing God's will is not out of your reach... in fact, it's wholly possible to know Him this well! Get ready to soar with God into new understandings of all He has for you! Choose to seek Him as you read *Discover God's Will.* Thom O'Leary delivers a flight you won't forget.

~ Kevin N. Springer

Foreword

Steve Sjogren
The Kindness Guy
Best Selling Author, *Conspiracy of Kindness*
www.Kindness.com

My wise grandma from Texas would have turned 100 years of age during the time I was writing this Foreword, so some of her witty sayings have come to mind. One of her great ones was, "There are two kinds of people in this world. Those who *can*, and those who *just flap their gums*." Thom O'Leary isn't much of a gum-flapper.

Thom has done the things that are written about in this book. He has cracked the code on understanding God's will in a way that will allow anyone who is spiritually open to see the best and highest God has for them.

In my experience as a pastor the main need for any of us boils down to this: to know the will of God. Once we have a clear sense of that, nearly everything else falls into place.

As some religious people argue over miniscule issues that are not going to make the slightest bit of difference in anyone's life, there is an amazing opportunity before us to connect with actors, musicians, bartenders, next-door neighbors—all sorts of people who are looking for God in the form of knowing His will for their lives. These are the sorts of people that may have a "clearly vague" misunderstanding about Christianity. It seems to me that if we can learn from this book and give away what we have learned we will be able to build some pretty amazing bridges to those who don't yet understand God.

Thom O'Leary has pulled off something that few authors have succeeded in doing over the years. He has managed to brilliantly handle the "sticky wicket" that many have tried to tackle but few have succeeded with.

Some books on guidance model exaggerations of the practicality of their message to the point that they cause the reader to dry up. On the other side are the books that are so overly spiritual that they cause the reader to blow up! Thom's book is a great balance between these two extremes. You won't dry up nor will you blow up, but in between you will grow up as you discover God's will for your life.

It's one thing to know that God has a plan for our lives, but it's a different matter to understand how to implement that plan. I've read a lot about how to get in touch with God's will for our lives. The problem is that sometimes the instructions are so step-by-step that it comes across as cold—

like a mathematical equation. Yes, there are lots of truths we ought to be aware of in terms of the mechanics of understanding the ways that God speaks. But none of those mechanics will do us any good if we are not walking in the Spirit.

As I read this book something began to happen in my heart and mind. I began to have what I now realize were "inspired ideas." This is one aspect of what the Apostle Paul talked about when he said we ought to "Walk in the Spirit." (Galatians 5:16, 25 KJV)

I hope this book gives you the same three gifts that it gave to me:

Encouragement

God breathed encouragement onto my heart and mind so that I could more clearly understand God's will for my life. I've been working on understanding God's will for my life for several decades—yes, decades—yet as I combed over this book I found some new arrows to put in my quiver.

Encouragement is contagious. Encouragement can come in a variety of ways, whether in the presence of a friend over a cup of coffee, through listening to someone speaking at a meeting, or in this case, reading the encouraging words of a person in a book.

I hope you are as encouraged in your discovery of God's will for your life as I was in mine.

Vision

We all need a 3-D view of things. If we are going to see with clarity we will need to understand more than just some words on a page. We need to put on our special glasses that will allow us to see images that jump off of the page.

God calls us to walk with a heart of humility that says, "I need help. I can't see the picture without help from Above." Thom's book helped me sharpen my vision.

Empowerment

This book gave me some important tools to help others on their quests to discover God's will. In our desires to reach out, let's see and be empowered in our opportunities to connect with the people in our networks, all of whom at some point are looking for God in the form of knowing His will for their lives.

~ Steve Sjogren

Dedication

Sherri O'Leary

You are my lover and my best friend. You know me more than anyone—and still choose to love *me*! I feel like we are on "the ride of a lifetime" that isn't even close to being over. I fell hard, head over heels when I saw you at age 17. I chased you through college. I'm the luckiest guy in the world. After 26 years of marriage, if I had to get married all over again—I'd pick you.

Brooke Ann (O'Leary) Jeffrey

Oh, my first born, sweet Brooke... let me begin by profusely apologizing for trying out my parenting skills on you! You have always been a princess to me—a graceful, quiet leader. You are so beautiful on the inside and out. (Man, Greg is a lucky man.) (I love you, Greg!)

Kate Grace O'Leary

Kait-lin! Oh, my, my... my dancer, my girl. You glow with beauty. You have the "it" factor. No one knows how to define that—however, you have it! Your love for Jesus, love for people, and love for those far from God, is AMAZING. Thanks for looking me square in the eyes when you were only 13 years old and "proclaiming" that I write a book. (Gosh, you were bold.)

Whitney Joy O'Leary

Whit, Whittie, Whittie-Whitster! Oh, my, my, my... third daughter of mine. You are a beautiful princess. Ever since you were born, people have said you were a firecracker, and that's not because you were born in July. However, I have always known that's because God has a huge plan for you. Your joyful heart and compassion for others take my breath away. I love listening to you sing. You rock my world, and you are incredible.

Luke Thomas O'Leary

My one and only son: let me begin with the words that you shouted at me as a toddler, "You the Man!" Luke, I am so proud of you. (I'm not going to lie; I'm also glad that you have brought testosterone to our female-filled family.) You are highly intelligent (4-point-something-something), athletic, confident, good looking, and tall! But your kindness expressed to others impresses me the most. God blessed me beyond my wildest dreams to give me a son like you. I love you so much.

To my family... this book is dedicated to you.

Table of Contents

Factor Three: The GOD and YOU Factor

Introduction

Everyone, deep down inside, wants to know God's will for his or her life.

Knowing God's will for my life: it's a universal longing for purpose and meaning, shared by anyone who looks at life for more than just existing day to day. Men and women struggle, wrestle, and get frustrated because they are unsure of where to turn or how to find out their purpose. I have personally met with thousands of people, and have found that there exists a deep longing within them to know God's will for their life.

Discover God's Will—Five Factors That Will Change Your Life Forever is a practical guide that helps an individual take steps to discover God's will. It's a dance. You are moving to the sound of the music, following the lead of your partner, yet not fully knowing where He will take you on the floor. You just trust Him.

This book delves deep into the heart of God and His will for us. It provides a path to run on that offers wisdom on how to discover God's plan for the future. It provides timeless truth, yet couched in mystery... it describes ageless principles and offers practical steps to take.

The book is founded in Holy Scripture, while written in a way that someone who doesn't know God could still "get it." More importantly, this book can launch people who do know God into their life-long calling, as well as their short-term mission.

Discover God's Will—Five Factors That Will Change Your Life Forever has the potential to be a catalyst for "life-change" for thousands and thousands of people. Perhaps you are one of them.

In these pages we will learn five key factors to knowing God's will:
1. **The YOU Factor**—Getting Ready to Hear God's Will
2. **The GOD Factor**—Five Ways God Speaks to Us
3. **The GOD and YOU Factor**—Receiving an Answer from God
4. **The TEST Factor**—Testing Your Decisions
5. **The PERSONAL Factor**—Walking It Out

While this book is written for everyone, the intended readership will be primarily people of faith. ***Discover God's Will—Five Factors That Will Change Your Life Forever*** is the first book in the Discover God Series—a series dedicated to helping multitudes of people get an answer from God that fulfills the longing of their hearts.

Based on random surveys that I have conducted over the years with my church members, it became very apparent to me that a longing to know God's will is a universal thread within most people. This book attempts to sew that up!

Pastoring a church of currently 1,500 people, and broadcasting a radio program that reaches thousands, I have had unique opportunities to get to see the longing of many people over a lot of years. As a pastor, I have connected with other churches, denominations, and movements, as well as my own church association, and have seen clear evidence of the overwhelming desire on the part of most people to know God's will for their lives.

It's a process of discovery. Interestingly, when one discovers God's will, he or she discovers God, and discovers him or her own self, too. I invite you to join me in this journey. Our lives will indeed be changed forever.

How to Use This Book

This book is structured around the Five Factors in five sections. I encourage you to read carefully through each section, and then pause, taking time to reflect and respond, applying the factor of that section to your life.

It will be helpful for you to write down and journal your thoughts. This will empower you in your pursuit of discovering God's will. Writing down responses will help you have clarity and give you opportunity to come back to your answers and reevaluate.

This book is a great resource for personal or group study. Your personal journey of discovering God's will is one that you alone will take, yet walking it out with others is powerful.

Factor One: The YOU Factor

Getting Ready

First Preparation: Understanding God's Will

"…be transformed by the renewing of your mind…"
Romans 12:2 (NIV)

Chapter 1

Decisions, Facing Forks in the Road

"Give us counsel, render a decision." Isaiah 16:3 (NIV)

The classic song from *Fiddler on the Roof* is, "Tradition." I find myself humming that song, changing the words from "Tradition, tradition! Tradition!" to "Decisions, decisions! Decisions!" There are always forks in the road of life that offer and demand important decision points.

Going into a new calendar year, many people look back and reflect on the previous year. I have traditionally taken the week between Christmas and New Year's to reflect and get vision. Most of my pursuits in a given year have flowed out of a yellow pad and pen, as I sit in my pajamas, in the wee hours of the morning, with a hot cup of coffee during this fabulous last week of December.

After reflecting on the past year, one can begin to look forward to the upcoming year. Yet as soon as you do that, you can almost hear the organ music playing in the background like in an old scary movie, "dun, dah, dun, dun, daaaah!" You are immediately and ultimately faced with choices. It is in that moment you have to boldly go where "only some" have gone before! You have to wrestle through those decisions, get God's heart, and pursue them like your life depended on it. There is no turning back.

> When you are facing choices, it is in that moment you have to boldly go where "only some" have gone before! You have to wrestle through those decisions, get God's heart, and pursue them like your life depended on it. There is no turning back.

Facing Choices

There are financial decisions we face that can make us cringe, "Cha-ching." Questions like, "What does God want me to do with my money? Where should I invest my money? Why is it that I don't have any money?!" Financial decisions are so critical because they deeply affect our lives and families. The last thing anyone wants is to make a wrong financial decision.

There are always decisions regarding relationships that need to be addressed, "How do I love this person who is driving me crazy when I'd rather listen to nails on a chalkboard than listen to them?" Questions like, "How do I do this relationship? What will it look like?" "Who is the right person for me?" arise in your mind.

Perhaps career decisions creep into your thoughts. It can be extremely tough trying to discern which job to take, or which one not to take. That is stressful. Then there are those times where you are faced with thinking, "Is it time for a career move?" That's a biggie.

If you are a parent, you will relate to this. If you are not a parent—just track this with me and it will shed light about how you were raised, and if you become a parent someday—you will thank me later. In parenting there is an ever-constant stream of meaningful decisions. Parental decisions are like Niagara Falls. I visited Niagara Falls one time and was overwhelmed by its power and constant flow. The bottom line is that you get the sense that this waterfall is never going to quit. Parents will have to embrace this. Just as Niagara Falls never stops, the flow of decisions never will either. Whether you like it or not, it's just true. And you will find that there are different kinds of decisions in every parenting season of life.

Parenting at the toddler stage comes with decisions, especially when the toddlers are learning their first two words (they are universal for every toddler by the way). The first one is, "No!" And the second word they learn is, "Mine!" As a parent your decision is, "How do I curb this innate selfishness?"

Then there is the child to early-adolescent stage, which can be fun and I have many fond memories of my kids in this stage. Oh there are issues that come up, but they are not as physically draining as the toddler years, and they sure as heck aren't as emotionally draining as the teenage years! Yet, in those early-adolescent years, there are decisions to be made and it takes a major effort of hands-on decisions, meaning, "Parents, don't you dare let go of that steering wheel!" During the adolescent years you have to make decisions that demonstrate you are the teacher and you are in control.

The latter-teenage years strike with a vengeance, and there are more critical decisions to be made. It doesn't have to be all bad, yet certainly there are those times when the temptation comes to look your teenager in the eye, and in the words of Bill Cosby, say, "I brought you into this world... and I can take you out!" When making parental decisions, especially with teenagers, I have a special prayer I use. I call it the "Oh God Prayer." It goes like this, "Oh God, Oh God, Oh God, Oh God, Oh God!" Try it some time; it's highly effective.

If you do not have children, you will ultimately have decisions to make in your life that will affect people around you. There will be friends, work associates, neighbors, and people in your sphere of influence that will be highly affected by the decisions you make, whether you recognize it or not. Reality says you will make decisions that absolutely affect your life. So whether you are single or married, or you are a student or a parent, you will make individual decisions that set your life in a certain direction. This drives home a sense of urgency, recognizing that the one thing you don't get back is time. You can make money, and you can make relationships, and you can do a lot of great things, yet truth be known, you and I cannot make time.

There exist critical and distinct seasons of life. Perhaps you have aging parents and all of sudden there is a role reversal. You are being dealt a brand new hand of cards and you're not sure how to play your hand. In fact, you would like the old deck of cards back! There are certain situations, hurdles and challenges of aging, which launch you into making really tough decisions about people you really care for.

This is where the rubber meets the road. In the heart of a believer there is a longing, "I want to do what God wants, and how God wants me to do it."

Some people will say, "Doesn't God want me to make choices?" Yes, absolutely He wants you to make choices. Or the question is asked, "Hasn't God given me free will to make decisions?" Yes, in fact, He has given you free will to make decisions. But ask this question as well, "Doesn't God, in His own heart and mind, know what is best?" Yes, that would be true as well. In the words of Perry Mason, or the television series Law and Order, depending on your generation, "Here is the verdict!" He is empowering you to make decisions, and in fact, He has something in mind that is best.

We Are On a Journey to Discover God's Will

Remember, we are on a journey to discover God's will. At the end of this journey, you are going to have the tools to understand what God's will is for those tough decisions you are facing. Also, remember that there is grace. God is not trying to fool you! And if you make the wrong decision, God has the uncanny ability to "re-direct" and "re-route" your decisions, just as a pilot can change his course in mid-flight. It would be like this, for example: "A private airplane was heading for San Francisco because of a decision that was made by the businessman passenger, and in mid-flight the pilot was notified that a heavy fog bank had drowned the San Francisco Airport. So, the pilot <u>re-directs</u> the businessman's decision to land in San Francisco, and lands in San Jose instead. The businessman then discovers that his meeting is actually being held in a town next to the San Jose airport." The businessman ended up having a change of direction, yet finds himself closer to his destination. God can re-direct and re-route your decisions, getting you closer to His perfect destination for you. The bottom line is, God's grace has you covered, make no mistake about it. God is just looking for hearts that want to fly and that have the attitude of Isaiah, "Here I am Lord, send me."

Preparation Mode: Get Ready

Knowing that God's grace has us covered, here is where we go into a preparation mode. There are so many great activities that call for the utmost, intense, focused preparation. It's all about getting ready.

Runners <u>get ready</u> by stretching out, breathing like they are in a Lamaze Class, "Woo, woo, woo!" They stretch, warm-up, and shake their legs like they have ants crawling on them. They are getting ready for the big race.

Ballet dancers <u>get ready</u> as they begin stretching. They then wrap their ankles and tighten their shoes just right for the big performance. I have a daughter who performs ballet on point (which means getting up on her toes, and how she does that is a marvel to me). It's fun to watch her warm up before performing, rehearsing every step and move in her head as she hums the music.

Football players, before the big game, <u>get ready</u>. They are putting on their pads, getting fired up for the battle, slapping each other's shoulder pads like hungry cannibals, and grunting like cavemen. (Having played college football myself, I'm afforded to use "caveman language" - and truth be known, football players reading this book are not offended, they actually like the comparison!)

Mountain climbers <u>get ready</u> as they review their equipment checklist: Backpack... "Check!" Water... "Check!" Power bars... "Check!" Toilet paper... "Check! Check! Check!" – That checklist is all about getting ready for the big climb.

Singers <u>get ready,</u> warming up their voices, mouthing really interesting words like "watermelon," moving up and down the music scale, getting those vocal chords primed to perform. Recently, I was at a ballgame, watching the young lady that was preparing to sing the National Anthem in front of thousands. She had a very serious face on, and was warming up her voice for the big song. Little did she know that the camera was on her and she was being broadcasted on the jumbo screen. I don't think she cared; she was getting ready.

Whether it's the big game, the big race, the big dance, the big climb, or the big song... we all get ready! When trying to find God's will, it all begins with "getting ready." Look at what Romans 12:2 says about getting ready through being renewed.

"Do not conform any longer to the pattern of this world, but <u>be transformed by the renewing of your mind</u>. Then you will be able

to test and approve <u>what God's will is</u>—His <u>good</u>, <u>pleasing</u> and <u>perfect will</u>."
(NIV; underlines added for emphasis)

Break Out of the Pattern the World Embraces

There is a pattern, a way of life or a standard of the world we live in. God says break out of that pattern! Don't do life according to that plan. In 1st Century Rome, when the Apostle Paul wrote this passage, there was a pattern that was the antithesis of the heart of God, where the weak were horrifically oppressed and atrocities were the norm. Perhaps you have seen the movie, *Gladiator*. It has a gripping story line and creates a vivid picture of the Roman-ruled world. The government held the people under oppression, soldiers were brutal and did as they pleased— regardless of the affect on others—and the people celebrated as prisoners killed one another, acting as though it was normal—as normal as watching the Super Bowl is to us.

It is also true that the 21st century that we live in has a pattern that the world embraces. This pattern says to be selfish versus being generous. It shouts to be a consumer versus being a contributor. The thought is, "Every man for himself," versus "Help all those you can!" God says to break out of that selfish worldly pattern, that self-absorbed rhythm of life, and instead choose His will.

Choose God's Will: Good, Pleasing, and Perfect

First, God's will is good for you. Whether a human being lived in the 1ˢᵗ Century Roman World, or is living in the 21ˢᵗ Century Western World, or anywhere in the world for that matter, when scripture says, "God has a <u>good</u> will," this simply means it's "gooooood!" Say that like a broadcaster as the football goes through the goal posts, "It's up, and it's gooooood!" God's will is never evil; it is never bad. Whatever is going on in your life, know that God has a good will and that He is not a God of oppression. Rather, His will for you is good through and through.

Secondly, God has a pleasing will, meaning it pleases Him, and satisfies Him. God likes His will and that means it's acceptable to Him. He is putting His stamp of approval on it. He accepts it. After all, it is His will.

Thirdly, God has a perfect will. This one's big -- think about this for a second. God has a perfect will for your life. He has a vision for your life, a preferred future for your life, and He has given us the gift to pursue His will... or run from it! (Note to self: See the story of Jonah. Jonah 1:3)

The first factor in discovering God's will for your life is what I call **The YOU Factor**. It begins with "you!" It begins inside of you. There is an inner-transformation that needs to take place. Or in other words, as Romans 12:2 says,

"...be transformed by the renewing of your mind." (NIV)

This transformation has to happen on the "inside" of you. It is a renewal that needs to take place in the deep pockets of your heart. Here it is... You as an individual have to be made ready to find God's will.

So we begin our path of discovering God's will... for you! Where do we turn? Let's turn to the number one thing Jesus told us to do.

Four Deep and Simple Truths

"[30] Love the Lord your God with all your <u>heart</u> and with all your <u>soul</u> and with all your <u>mind</u> and with all your <u>strength</u>.' [31] The second is this: 'Love your neighbor as yourself.' There is no commandment greater than these."
Mark 12:30-31
(NIV; underlines added for emphasis)

There are four deep, and yet simple truths that God calls us to. These truths have to do with our Heart, Mind, Soul and Strength. Now think this through with me. The end result is to know God's will—so the start of our trek means we need to personally get ready. "<u>Getting ready</u>" <u>means preparing yourself</u>.

Let's continue our journey in knowing God's will and the first factor, **The YOU Factor**, and begin in Chapter 2 where Jesus began... with the heart.

> "<u>Getting ready</u>" <u>means preparing yourself</u>.

Factor One: The YOU Factor

Getting Ready
Second Preparation: Your Heart

Chapter 2
Preparing Your Heart

"Test me, O LORD, and try me, examine my heart."
Psalms 26:2 (NIV)

Whether you resonate with the preparation of a dancer, a singer, a football player, a runner, or a mountain climber, it's time to get ready for the big game, the big race, the big dance, the big climb, or the big song. We are after knowing God's will and it requires preparation of the heart. It is time to prepare yourself, literally at the core of who you are, and the core of who you are, is what the Bible calls your "heart."

Preparing Your Heart—Your Spiritual Core

We must start with the CORE of you and work outward. When the Bible speaks of your heart, it is not talking about the organ that pumps blood through your veins.

A friend of mine walked into a room and secretly observed his seven-year-old boy who had recently invited Jesus into his heart. His son was looking down at his chest, literally talking to his heart, "Jesus, I know you are in there now. I'm not sure how you fit in there, but I asked you into my heart, so I know you are there." I love the honesty of kids!

When you read the word *heart*, it is talking about the very spiritual essence and core of who you are. The Psalmist wrote in Psalm 66:18,

> "If I had cherished sin in my heart, the Lord would not have listened." (NIV)

The Psalmist knew an important reality. If you desire sin, God can't listen to your prayer. Now, there is a huge difference between working on getting rid of bad habits, wrong thoughts, misguided attitudes, ignorant actions, and plain old sin, versus maintaining an internal state of rebellion that says, "It's my life and I will do as I please!"

Or in the words of the famous theologian Frank Sinatra, "I did it my way!" If that's where you are coming from, then you don't really need to know God's will because you are going to do whatever you want.

On the other hand, if you are saying, "God, I really want to do what is right. Give me the strength and the guidance." Well, God answers that type of prayer.

Let me remind you that we all have made mistakes. We all have come up short. No one is perfect and no one bats a thousand! Truth be known, most people try hard to do good and yet we all make mistakes.

There once was a guy who knew he had tried hard and yet made a mistake. He was at the gates of heaven and Saint Peter was there to greet him, and asked, "Before I let you in can you tell me any act of goodness that you ever did?" The guy said, "Well one time I saw an elderly lady being mugged by a motorcycle gang, so I jumped right in and knocked over their Harley Davidsons. I then threw myself in between three guys and fought them with all my might! Having done that courageous good deed, the elderly lady was able to escape with her life!" Saint Peter said, "That's marvelous! How long ago was that?" The guy said, "Uh, about five minutes ago." Can you say, "Dead-O!"?

Just like this guy, you can attempt to do good deeds and try hard to do good things. To be clear, doing good things is good, yet it doesn't get you into heaven. <u>God is after your heart</u>. I tell my church all the time, "Good things are good. Feeding the poor is good. Serving in ministry is good. Being really nice to your pastor is GOOD! REALLY GOOD!! But that doesn't get you into heaven."

Healing a Dislocated Heart

God desires your heart to be whole, and it is also true that life has ups and downs; it has hurts and heartaches and no one is immune to life's pain. And these hurts can affect our hearts along the way of life. In fact it can make our hearts get bumped out of place. Because of life's knocks, our hearts can get dislocated.

When I was playing football at Cal Poly back in the eighties we were in spring training and I took an excruciating hit to my shoulder (from some demonic linebacker, but that's another story!). The hit was a cheap shot that spun me around like a spinning top. I came up out of it in a complete daze, not even knowing where I was. It took me about ten minutes of glazed eyes, looking up at the Cal Poly clock tower, to finally figure out that I was at Cal Poly and in spring training for football. Now you may not be a football fan, or a person who doesn't like sports so much, but feel my pain here with some compassion! I took a hit and the result was a dislocated shoulder. I couldn't even lift my arm up (okay, I confess… now I'm looking for the sympathy card).

Yet, track this: there was a hit… and it lead to a dislocation… an out-of-joint part… something that had been connected, in place, and functioning the way it was designed to function, but now out of place. Our hearts are the exact same way. Life serves up hits, sometimes cheap shots, things happen to us out of our control and the by-product can be a heart that is dislocated. Since we are passionately after preparing our hearts, we need to make sure that we can get our hearts back into the place they were designed to be.

That's why Proverbs 4:23 warns us,

> "Above all else, guard your heart, for everything you do flows from it." (NIV)

This presents the wisdom that all issues of life flow in and through our hearts.

So if we are honest, we understand that our hearts are fragile and can take excruciating hits along the way of life—which can immensely affect our ability to discern God's will for our lives. Sometimes it is from the wrongs we've done, and sometimes it is from the wrongs done to us that our hearts become dislocated.

God wants to heal your dislocated heart. If your heart is out of place, out of joint, God can get it back into the right place.

Proverbs, the book of wisdom that aides us in navigating through life, also reminds us in Chapter 13, verse 12,

"Hope deferred makes the heart grow sick." (NIV)

Hoping for something means it hasn't happened. There are so many life events that can make a heart grow sick. That could mean physical problems you are enduring, or emotional hurts that have not been healed. It could mean a spiritual attack that you have suffered. Our hearts can grow sick because of financial pressures we face, or even relational breakdowns that leave us numb.

No matter what you are going through, you may have asked yourself, "Can I get my heart re-connected to God and to others?" And the answer is, "Yes, yes you can."

Reconnecting your heart to God and healing a dislocated heart, is all a part of PREPARING YOUR HEART to know

God's will. That's why factor one is **The YOU Factor**... getting yourself ready to hear from God.

The Psalmist proclaimed in Psalm 34:18,

> "The LORD is <u>close to the brokenhearted</u>
> and saves those who are crushed in spirit."
> (NIV; underline added for emphasis)

This is good news. God heals broken and dislocated hearts.

God heals broken and dislocated hearts.

In the Old Testament God was given descriptive names, one being "Jehovah Rapha" which means, "God, my Healer." God comes close to the brokenhearted and restores the crushed in spirit. Remember, our hearts are our spiritual core and only God can perform surgery there.

Have you ever gotten the wind knocked out of you? It's the worst. It's that phenomena where you get hit so hard — you can't breathe! I was one of those accident-prone kids. Just ask my Mom. At eight years old, I fell out of a 30-foot-plus tree and lived to tell about it! My folks were always getting phone calls from the local school, "Thom got hurt again." This became a regular routine. I was a passionate kid, and whether it was playing kickball or four-square on the playground I would run into poles, people, or buildings. I was always getting banged up. I remember the school principal telling me, "Thom, I think you're accident prone." My response was, "You think?" I remember being in an intense kickball game on the elementary school playground. I was chasing down the ball and turned around only to run right into a pole. I vividly remember getting the wind knocked out me. Your eyes get really big, you can't speak, even if you try, and you just kind of stare out into space until you can get your breath back.

As a pastor, seeing literally thousands of people every week, this is what I know. Many of you reading this book have "spiritually gotten the wind knocked out of you." In fact, you can't really even talk about it, since you are spiritually gasping for air. No matter what caused it, you have to come to God just as you are with your hurts, habits, and hang-ups, and invite God into that place because you need to breathe again.

You have got to let God give you your breath back. He's close to you, more than you know. Open your heart to Him. You may need to meet with a really good counselor, pastor, or a close friend to help in the healing process. This is how it works... He comes close and then He brings strength and healing.

I love the words of the Psalmist in Psalm 73 that remind us:

"My flesh and my heart may fail, but God is the <u>strength of my heart</u> and my portion forever." (Psalm 73:26)
(NIV; underline added for emphasis)

It is so true that along the way of life we have these great highs and great lows that affect our spiritual core, the heart. Life can be like a rollercoaster ride and there are times where you feel like collapsing physically or emotionally, even spiritually. But the Lord is always near, He's always with us, and we need to remind ourselves of this truth constantly.

When one of my daughters was a little younger, we went to a popular amusement park in Southern California. She begged me to take her on a particular roller coaster, the biggest one of the whole park. We stood in line for what seemed to be half the day. It was finally our turn. We stepped into the roller coaster car, buckled in, and it immediately pulled forward to start the ride. My young innocent daughter looks at me and says, "I don't want to do this after all." "Excuse me?" I wasn't sure I heard her correctly. "I don't want to do this after all," she said with all seriousness. I then said, "Honey, it's too late. We are buckled in and ready to take off." She then, kid you not, clasped her hands, bowed her head, and launched into a very passionate prayer that went like, "Dear Lord, please don't let me die. Amen." All of sudden the roller coaster took off at what felt like Mach speed. My daughter began to scream at the top of her lungs at every turn, corner and corkscrew, "OH, JESUS!!!!! OH, GOD!!!!!" She repeated again and again, "OH, JESUS!!!!! OH, GOD!!!!!" We finally made it to the end with my daughter dramatically demonstrating thanksgiving to the Almighty, "Thank you, God, thank you, God." After we got off of the roller coaster and walked out the exit, someone asked me, "How was it?" I said, "I don't know, but my daughter just met Jesus!"

Here's the deal: life can be like a roller coaster ride, filled with wild ups and downs, and we cry out passionately to God as we are flung at what feels like warp speed. That ride can take a toll on our hearts. Yet, remember God is the strength of your heart and your portion forever. That means your life is in His hands... forever. So you don't need to worry, or stress. He's in control. God comes close, bringing healing and strength.

It is interesting that Jesus said,

> "Blessed are the pure in heart, for they will
> <u>see</u> God." Matthew 5:8
> (NIV; underline added for emphasis)

When your heart is put back in place and is truly right where it needs to be, you will have spiritual eyes to see God working in your life, and you will be better able to discern His will.

Knowing the condition of our heart is a vital aspect in knowing God's will. Jesus talked about some people later in the book of Matthew and about what had happened to their hearts…

> "For this people's heart has become <u>calloused</u>; they hardly hear with their ears, and they have closed their eyes. Otherwise they might see with their eyes, hear with their ears, understand with their hearts and <u>turn</u>, and <u>I would heal them</u>." Matthew 13:15
> (NIV; underlines added for emphasis)

Because of life's hurts, your heart can become calloused, and if it does, you can miss out on the life that God has for you. Jesus said, "turn." That means, in your heart a shift needs to take place. Do a 180-degree turn at the core of who you are. That shift empowers you to take that dislocated heart and put it back in place. It means, you turn to Him and He will heal you.

Preparing an Authentic Heart

Part of getting ready to hear God's will and <u>preparing your heart</u> means cultivating an authentic heart. Sincerity, honesty, and authenticity are critical.

Romans 12:9 says,

> "Love must be <u>sincere</u>. Hate what is evil;
> cling to what is good."
> (NIV; underlines added for emphasis)

Your love must be real. Your heart must be real. And while it is being sincere, hate evil and hang on to what is good—like your life depends on it.

Your love must be real. Your heart must be real. And while it is being sincere, hate evil and hang on to what is good—like your life depends on it.

Scripture says, "cling." The word *cling* denotes the act of gluing, or uniting firmly by glue. Have you ever seen the poster with a cat hanging onto a ball of yarn and the statement underneath that says, "Hang on baby—help is on the way!" Well, hang onto what is good, right, and true and get your claws so dug into what is right that you don't let go!

Knowing that your heart is your spiritual core, it is interesting that the Old Testament Hebrew word for heart is *lehv*, which means your "life source." This Hebrew word for your heart literally translates as "the wellspring of life— your inner yearnings." Therefore, it is a high calling to protect your heart, and to not allow that "wellspring" to get tainted.

If we let evil or negative things into our lives, and into our hearts, they begin to taint our ability to hear from God. At the same time, those tainted things affect what comes flowing out of our lives. So scripture emphatically says, "Love must be <u>sincere</u>." That means, while you are living in a synthetic, fake world, be radically authentic.

Sir Arthur Conan Doyle, the author of *Sherlock Holmes*, was known to be quite a prankster. As a joke, he sent ten of his friends, who were all upper class nobles in London, an anonymous note. All that the note said was, "ALL HAS

BEEN FOUND OUT—LEAVE AT ONCE!" In the morning he found out that all ten had fled the country! These ten friends were probably not as authentic as people thought.

The heart principle is, "Don't be fake, don't hide things, and be the real deal." God sees your life through and through. You can't fool God. It's like a musician. You can't fake it. When you stand up to play, whatever comes out of your instrument is real. It may be really good music and it may be downright awful. However, it's authentic.

Healing a Painful Heart

In preparing our hearts to hear God's will for our lives, we have discussed healing a dislocated heart and cultivating an authentic heart. Another step in preparing our hearts is healing a painful heart, which requires testing our hearts.

We have a hot tub that our family has enjoyed over the years. In fact, some of our greatest family times have been gazing at the stars, calling time-out on life, and connecting with one another at a heart level. Maintaining this hot tub means that the water has to be tested and treated! Just like I test the water with a pH stick, and see how the chlorine is doing, so we have to check the "pH" of our hearts. Sometimes when we test our hearts we find horrific pain, which hinders us in discovering God's will.

As we have discussed, our hearts can accumulate pain. Preparing our hearts to know God's will, means getting through the pain of life. Authors Bill Donahue and Russ Robinson relate the words of Lyman Coleman as he worked through the pain in his heart and reflected on the death of his beloved wife, Margaret:

> "The most painful decision of my life was asking God to take her home. She had been suffering from repeated brain seizures and her body was wasted. I whispered in her ear: 'Honey, I love you. I love you. Jesus wants you to come home. We are going to be all right. We give you permission to let go.' She closed her eyes and fell asleep...
>
> "As I write this letter, I realize I am without my editor. My greatest critic. My teammate. Soulmate. Prayermate. Partner in everything. We traveled the roads less traveled together in hard times and good times. Honey, I miss you. I miss you. I miss you. I will keep the light on for the kids. I will be there for friends. And one day, we are going to join you. All of us. Because Jesus promised it. 'Precious in the sight of the Lord is the death of his saints.'"

No matter what disappointment we have endured, as we open our hearts to the healing of Jesus, the pain lifts and our hearts get pure and clear to hear God's will. This is all a part of preparing our hearts and getting ready.

Preparing a Passionate Heart

The final preparation of our hearts is getting the fire back. There is nothing like getting your heart ablaze with passion. The number one thing that can set your heart on fire is the love of Christ.

When you get that passion in your heart, it changes your life for good and prepares you to hear God's will. That is what happens when you die to the old life. Though to be sure, every so often the old life or what I would call the "old man," you know what I mean—the old man, the old person you used to be—raises its head and you need to knock it back down. You need to proclaim, "I'm not that person anymore!"

Preparing your heart to hear God's will means that you have to cultivate a passionate heart. Pain can affect your heart. Being empty of passion can affect your heart as well. It is also true that being in the grind of life and suffering through the mundane can rip off our hearts from getting prepared to hear God's will.

Whether your heart has been damaged or you are lost in transition, you need to know God is in the business of changing lives. If your heart is dislocated and out of joint, God can put your heart back together again, but you have to ask Him to. I laughed at the bumper sticker, "Humpty-Dumpty was pushed!" It is true, we have people in our lives that hurt our hearts, yet God can put the pieces back together again.

Here's good news. God says, "Come to me with an honest heart." You do that by coming just as you are and saying, "Lord, here are my struggles. I want to do better. Please help me and change me." Then you allow Christ to cleanse and forgive you of a guilty conscience, and of things you have done that you know were wrong.

When you come to Jesus at a heart level, he does three things for you. First, He forgives your past—your past is forgiven. Second, He gives you a purpose for living. And third, He offers the hope of heaven. Think of those three important words: forgiven, living, and heaven. They grab a hold of your past, present, and future.

> Whether your heart has been damaged or you are lost in transition, you need to know God is in the business of changing lives.

God changes our hearts, as my friend, Eddie Espinosa, experienced. He was driving down the back roads in Southern California a number of years ago. As Eddie began contemplating the purity of God and the depravity of man (more specifically himself), the words to a song, "Change My Heart, Oh God" began to pour from his heart and he began to sing,

> *"Change my heart oh God, make it ever true, change my heart, oh God, may I be like you. You are the potter I am the clay. Mold me and make me. This is what I pray."*

Now Christians in countless churches all over the world sing that song because one man cried out to God in his car on a back road in Southern California.

God answers prayers like that! That's the kind of prayer that the Lord desires to answer. He will meet you right where you are. I remember a mentor of mine telling me, "Man can change his mind, yet only God can change the heart." That simply means we have to choose to open our hearts to God and ask Him to change them. And He will.

So the first step in "getting ready" is to <u>prepare your heart</u>. After getting your heart in the right place, by turning to God, asking for forgiveness, being honest with your weakness, and trusting in the power of Christ, you can now take the next step from the heart. We now journey into our minds, scary I know, but necessary nonetheless.

Factor One: The YOU Factor

Getting Ready
Third Preparation: Your Mind

Chapter 3
Readying Your Mind

"Letting the Spirit control your mind leads to life and peace." Romans 8:6 (NLT)

Part of knowing God's will is winning a battle! And that battle is going on "right between your ears!" There is a famous sports announcer that has a signature statement when a professional basketball player hits a big three-point shot. The announcer roars as the basketball swishes through the net, "Right between the eyes!" Well, let me make this crystal clear with more fiery passion than a sportscaster, our battle is "Right between the ears!" The battlefield is, in fact, in our minds. Get this one right and you are on your way to knowing God's will. So much can happen in our minds that shape the way we interact with God. It can influence the way we hear God. It simply affects our relationship with God.

Our minds are so powerful. And like a battlefield, there are bombs going off everywhere. Thoughts explode in our minds and can trigger deep emotions. Yet, it is God's intention that you would win the battle. Because every action, good or bad, you have ever done was originated from a thought. The questions become, "What are the prevailing thoughts in my mind?" "What do I think about day in and day out?" "What consumes my thought life?"

We have to be mentally prepared to hear from God. Therefore, let's focus on preparing our minds.

Preparing Your Mind—Your Thought Life

Scripture tells us in 1 Peter 1:13,

> "Therefore, <u>prepare your minds for action</u>; be self-controlled; set your hope fully on the grace to be given you when Jesus Christ is revealed."
> (NIV; underline added for emphasis)

Here we are talking about preparing ourselves to be able to know God's will and 1 Peter calls us to "prepare your minds for action." This kind of preparation will come by being self-controlled in your mind, being hopeful in your mind, and being focused on the Lord in your mind.

Self-control

Being self-controlled in your mind is a huge element in hearing from God. Your mind can take you anywhere and everywhere. You have to pull in the reins when it comes to being self-controlled in your mind. It's like the cowboy who said he had two horses. One horse wanted to run toward what is righteous and the other horse wanted to run toward evil. When asked which horse wins, the cowboy replied, "Whichever one I say 'giddy-up' to!"

Isn't it true? We can allow our minds to take us in a direction where we never thought we would go. Yet if we were honest, we would recognize that we have the power to say, "Giddy-up!" We also have the power to say, "Whoa!" That's what it means to have a self-controlled mind. When your thoughts begin to take off in the wrong direction, pull back, and stop that thought track.

Centered around Hope

It is also equally important to have your mind and thoughts centered around hope! Hope is such a driving force in our lives, and dwelling on thoughts that make you hopeful is downright powerful.

Having thoughts of hope lead you in the right direction. God is the God of hope and desires that you would lead a life of hope. For that to happen, your mind must be filled with thoughts of hope.

Keep Him on the Forefront of Your Mind

While seeking God's will for your life, it will require keeping Him on the forefront of your mind. Let's face it. We think about what we care about. Begin to think about God. Let your thoughts be filled with His thoughts. Let your prayer be, "God, whatever You care about, help me to care about. Whatever breaks Your heart, break my heart. Whatever You think about, let me think about."

There have been moments in my life when I'm driving in my car at a crazy time, when most people are sleeping, like 3:00 a.m. or 4:00 a.m. and there are no other cars around. And I will simply talk to God, saying, "Lord, I don't if anyone is praising You right now in my town, but I am right now. So whatever You are concerned about, help me to be concerned about!" God can hear millions of prayers all at the same time. God is omnipresent and nothing is too big for Him. However, He desires that we are personal with Him. He also wants us to invite "His control" over our lives.

Romans 8:6 gives an incredible insight in preparing your mind,

> "If your sinful nature controls your mind, there is death. But if the <u>Holy Spirit controls your mind</u>, there is life and peace."
> (NLT; underline added for emphasis)

If your sinful nature is controlling your mind, then you die spiritually on the inside. "Death" means "separation from God." So, how will you be able to know God's will if you are distant from Him, or dead to Him!? However, there is life and peace on the inside when the Holy Spirit controls your mind. There is pure creativity and a quiet confidence when the Holy Spirit is controlling your mind. There is inspiring vision and a holy calmness when the Holy Spirit is controlling your mind. There are endless possibilities and a settled mind that "God is in control" when the Holy Spirit is controlling your mind.

I want to teach you a five-word prayer based on Romans 8:6. You can pray it when you get up in the morning, when you are at work, on your coffee break, at lunch time, and even driving home, watching TV, or going to bed. That five-word prayer that will change your life is, "HOLY SPIRIT, CONTROL MY MIND."

Whatever thoughts that are going on in your mind, and are controlling your thought-life, absolutely will affect your "getting ready" to know God's will. I encourage you to memorize Philippians 4:8 which talks about what should go on between your ears:

> "Whatever is true, whatever is noble, whatever is right, whatever is pure, whatever is lovely, whatever is admirable—if anything is excellent or praiseworthy—think about such things." (NIV; underline added for emphasis)

This verse is saying that everything that is good, right, and true in life, we should think about those things! We should fill our minds with these things. There is a high call to let these types of thoughts be the objects of our attention to the point that we would study them, and even practice them. Think about what these types of thoughts are, and then think on the high call to observe those thoughts. Begin to think on how these thoughts will influence you and how they would influence the world around you.

Because whatever you think about is what you are going to do! As we discussed, our actions originate in our minds. The person who goes out and robs a bank did not just walk into the bank to make a deposit and say, "Oh, by the way, I'm robbing your bank right now, please put the cash in the bag!" No, that is not what happened. In fact the bank robber thought about it for days, even weeks. The person that finds their self in adultery may say to himself or herself, "I can't believe this happened." Truth be known, the thought was in their mind long ago. No one wakes up one day and says, "I'm going to commit adultery today!" The thought was ruminating in the walls of their mind for weeks, months, even years.

On the flip side, positive things that are done, like showing mercy to the poor, begins with thinking about what is noble. A person begins to consider, "What is noble?" The thought comes to mind that, "Helping others is noble." The person says to himself or herself, "I want to be that type of person, a noble person who helps those in need." Even the positive, life-changing things we do, originate in a single thought.

… whatever you think about is what you are going to do!

Jesus said the greatest thing you could do is love God with your heart, mind, soul and strength. So how do you love God with your mind? Think about such things that are listed in Philippians 4:8! Think about what is true, noble, right, pure, lovely, and admirable—anything that is excellent or praiseworthy.

Have you ever watched a movie that impacted you so much that the images stayed in your mind permanently? A friend once shared with me how she had watched the movie *Werewolf* as a young teenager. This was the first scary movie she had ever seen and some of the images stayed with her permanently. She is now in her forties and she can still vividly recall the claws of the werewolf coming through the roof of the car! She admits that she replayed particular scenes in her mind over and over after she watched the movie, even though they frightened her. Isn't this what we catch ourselves doing in life?

We play that <u>argument</u> over and over and rehearse what we should have said. We play the <u>negative</u> <u>comments</u> over and over when someone criticizes us harshly. We beat ourselves up for the <u>sins</u> of the past. We essentially build a library of negative DVDs that often get set to "continuous replay!" Those negative DVDs are filled with bad thoughts, negative experiences, the wrongs we've done, the wrongs done to us—and we replay them over and over again on the TV screen of our minds.

Exchange Negative Thoughts with What God Says about You

You have to exchange those negative DVD's with positive DVD's in your mind, that is, what God says about you. Make the exchange! Trade in those fights and arguments for thoughts of grace, mercy and forgiveness. Trade in those negative comments from the coach, parent, teacher, boss, and the "so-called" friend for the positive comments that God says about you! His Word says that you are "loved with an everlasting love... that you are His child... that you are His beloved... that before the beginning of the world He was thinking about you!" Make the great exchange of the old DVD's for the good, right, and true DVD's that should play in your mind.

What about bad thoughts that pop into my mind? Any one of us can be going through our day and have the strangest thought fly right through our minds. I heard a pastor quote the famous preacher Charles Spurgeon and this little gold nugget of wisdom has helped me immensely and

﹍ne deeper insight, stating, "I can't control crows ﹍ying over my head, but I don't have to let them nest in my hair." That simply means that you and I cannot control a bad thought from flying through our minds, but on the other hand we don't have to hang onto it, dwell on it, that is, let it nest in our heads!

The "Five-Second" Rule

I call it the "Five-Second" rule. In reality, you have about five seconds to shoo those crows out of your mind before they start to nest! If you let a bad thought nest for more than five seconds, you're in trouble. That is when one thought leads to another, and to another, and then to another. You may think, "How could I ever be thinking about this?" However, it all started in the first five seconds. We have five seconds to shoo those crows and bad thoughts out of our minds or we are in for some trouble. Ultimately that trouble could mean missing out on God's message to us. And if we miss His message, we miss His will.

Preparing your mind is critical to discovering God's will for your life. It takes serious focus to get your mind filled with the thoughts that position you into the place of hearing God's voice in your life. Doesn't it make sense? If you are longing for God's thoughts, then you need "God-thoughts" to be flooding your mind. There are so many distractions, and our minds have the propensity to wander. I encourage you to get super serious with your thought life. If you want to know God's will, you have to.

Preparing your mind is critical to discovering God's will.

Once your heart has become honest with God, and your mind has become clear, you can move forward. Let us continue on to boldly go where everyone needs to go... the soul!

Factor One: The YOU Factor
Getting Ready
Fourth Preparation: Your Soul

Chapter 4
Priming Your Soul

"What good is it for a man to gain the whole world, yet forfeit his soul?" Mark 8:36 (NIV)

I was walking through an airport years ago when I saw a bookstand promoting the best-selling book, *Chicken Soup for the Soul*. The title certainly caught my eye, as I had never heard of the book. As a kid I grew up on chicken soup, and loved it. As a pastor, the word "soul" is obviously meaningful, so I immediately started thumbing through the book, not realizing how wildly popular it would become.

People certainly resonate with the need to heal their soul. It is so true that we need to take care of our soul and allow God to bring comfort to our inner-person. Yet, we have to really understand what our soul actually is, and what it is not.

When the Bible speaks of your soul, it is proclaiming that your soul is made up primarily of three parts. Those three parts include your mind (what you think about), your will (what you choose to do or the decisions you make) and your emotions (how you feel). All three of these—mind, will, and emotions—play huge parts in understanding the will of God for your life. So let's get a better understanding of our souls.

What Makes Up Your Soul?

Your <u>MIND</u>—The thoughts and memories you hold on to

Each one of us has thoughts that dominate our minds. Those thoughts are powerful. Our minds can be filled with so many different kinds of thoughts. Thoughts that are bad or good, sad or glad. There are memories we hold onto from the past. Those memories can be either great highlights or horrible regrets. Truth be known, we are going to be thinking about something. In fact Philippians 4:8 gives a short list of the type of thoughts that should fill our minds (from the last chapter):

"Whatever is true, whatever is noble, whatever is right, whatever is pure, whatever is lovely, whatever is admirable—if anything is excellent or praiseworthy—<u>think about such things</u>." Philippians 4:8
(NIV; underline added for emphasis)

This verse is saying that everything that is good, right, and true—think about those things. Fill your mind with these types of thoughts. Let them become the objects of your attention and study them, and practice them. Think about the effect of those thoughts ruminating in your mind. Think on the high call to observe them. Even think about the influence which they would have on the world around you. Thoughts are powerful!

As we discussed in chapter three, whatever we think about is what we are going to do. Your actions originate in your mind.

Biblically, part of your soul is your mind, and the thoughts and memories you hold onto. Every so often I will have a thought that surfaces as a flashback from when I was only five years old. Amazingly, that thought is over 40 years old and has lingered in my soul.

In addition to your mind, another part of your soul is your will.

Your <u>WILL</u>—The decisions you make

Your will, the things you choose, the decisions you make, are parts of an internal process. We all choose what we are going to do. That's part of the on-going workings of your soul. In the Old Testament Joshua made a great statement about choosing.

> "But if serving the LORD seems un-desirable to you, then <u>choose for yourselves</u> this day whom you will serve... But as for me and my household, we will serve the LORD."
> Joshua 24:15
> (NIV; underline added for emphasis)

I love the honesty of Joshua as he is talking to his people. He calls upon the people to make their choice, because God himself would not force them. Joshua knew they must serve the Lord with all their heart, if they were to serve him at all. So he states that for himself and his family—this is what we are doing. He shows the people around him that his personal, individual choice was already fixed. It was a done deal. There was no argument. He was not pointing fingers nor judging. However, he knew what he and his family were doing. Joshua and his family had taken the LORD for their portion—for their life.

Making choices, that is choosing or your will, comes from the soul. Someone can say, "I'm choosing to be kind, or I'm choosing to be mean." Those choices are flowing out of your inner-person, your soul.

I was recently at a football game and someone yelled at me, using language that included four-letter words that I cannot repeat. My son was with me in this awkward moment. For a split second, like .3 of a second, I wanted to punch the guy. Then the rest of that second—.7—flashed before my eyes: the newspaper headline of the next day, "PASTOR STARTS BRAWL AT BALL GAME!" That is not the press I'm looking for! So I smiled at the individual and went on my way. I don't always get it right, yet that was a good choice.

Your choices—your actions resulting from decisions you will make—are major parts of your inner person, your soul. Biblically, your mind and will make up your soul along with the third part, your emotions.

Your <u>EMOTIONS</u>—The feelings you experience on the inside

Emotions and feelings are such huge parts of your inner person, or your soul. God created you that way—to feel. He created you to sense joy and to sense sadness, to know excitement and to know pain. We are created with this emotional make-up that is good. And the more your soul is healthy, the more your emotions will be healthy.

The Apostle Paul is writing to the church in Philippi and he shows he cares about them in a big way. We have to understand that Paul is a "man's-man." If Paul had ever taken a personality test, he would be on the top of the chart as the highly driven one! Paul is one that would say things like, "I have purpose in every step... I land my punches... I'm running to win the race." Yet in Philippians 1:7 he talks about his "feelings." So don't think that feelings are bad, or unneeded, or wimpy.

> "It is right <u>for me to feel this way</u> about all of you, since <u>I have you in my heart</u>; for whether I am in chains or defending and confirming the gospel, all of you share in God's grace with me." Philippians 1:7
> (NIV; underlines added for emphasis)

Paul is saying, "I have the warmest love for you. I have the most affectionate memories of you. I have intense feelings about you." Why? Because he had them in his heart and soul.

God created you to feel. And as you let the Lord restore your soul—which is a promise from Psalm 23, to remake your soul, renovate your soul, re-establish your soul, and repair your soul—you will begin to have the right kinds of feelings.

I was saying good-bye to my daughter in the San Francisco Airport, as she was leaving for six months to work with a Christian organization internationally. As I was saying goodbye I was balling my eyes out! In the words of Apostle Paul, "I have a right to feel this way!" I'm her daddy and it's my right. Feelings are powerful.

Since we are still in preparation mode, we have to understand the magnitude of how our emotional well-being affects knowing the will of God for our lives. Because if your emotions are in the dumps, it will be really difficult to discern God's will. It's like when you are sick and grumpy, your attitude says, "I don't want to talk to anyone, just leave me alone! Don't even touch me!" If your soul is in that condition, then you are in trouble. So it is vital to be emotionally well, where you are not grumpy toward God!

He will not force Himself on you or knock down your door. If you don't want to talk to Him, He will simply wait for you.

…we have to understand the magnitude of how our emotional well-being affects knowing the will of God for our lives. Because if your emotions are in the dumps, it will be really difficult to discern God's will.

Preparing Your Soul — Your Emotional Well-being

Scripture gives us very powerful instruction for daily living in 1 Thessalonians 5:16-18,

> "Be joyful always; pray continually; give thanks in all circumstances, for <u>this is God's will</u> for you in Christ Jesus."
> (NIV; underline added for emphasis)

God's will for us is to be joyful, prayerful, and thankful— no matter what! That is a tall order, yet it is the target on the wall. We all feel sadness, or fear, or other emotions, but the goal is to learn to be joyful, prayerful, and thankful, which gets us ready to hear from God.

God's Universal Will and His Specific Will

In knowing God's will, it is critical to realize that there are two dimensions: His universal will and His specific will. His universal will refers to what He calls all of us to do, and His specific will means what He has for you personally. But if you don't know or do His universal will, you won't be able to discover His specific will.

Because of that, it would be wise to follow the instructions of 1 Peter 2:11,

> "Dear friends, I urge you, as aliens and strangers in the world, to abstain from sinful desires, <u>which war against your soul</u>."
> (NIV; underline added for emphasis)

> ...the goal is to learn to be joyful, prayerful, and thankful, which gets us ready to hear from God.

The Battle for Your Soul Comes in Three Waves

Once again there is a battle going on... a battle for your soul! This battle wars against your mind, will, and emotions.

This particular battle comes in three waves. One wave is your own *sinful nature*. The second wave is *the influence of the world* we live in. And the third wave is *spiritual warfare* as described in Ephesians 6, depicting the enemy of your soul.

Our *sinful nature* can take us anywhere and we have to "die to it" daily. When thinking about your soul in the three parts of mind, will, and emotions, you can quickly identify how our sinful nature can operate. Sin originates in our minds. We get a crazy thought, or what I like to call a stupid thought that leads to a crossroad. The crossroad is one of making a decision. Now it is your will that decides which direction you are going to go. We all make mistakes; no one is perfect, no one bats a thousand. However, the more that we can align our mind, will, and emotions with God, the more we are going to discover His will for our lives.

The second wave of *influence comes from the world*. It's all around us! There are so many "messages" being played every day on TV, radio, computers, magazines and newspapers. And to be clear, many of those messages are warring against your soul. The message may be temptation, and it may simply be a distraction. Yet, the tragedy is when we allow ourselves to get distracted and our souls end up being drawn away from the whispers of God.

The third wave of *spiritual warfare* is the tricky one. Scripture lets us know that we have this invisible battle going on. People will ask me, "How does that work?" I like to think of radio waves. I can't see radio waves, but they are still very real. They zip right through our bodies without us knowing it. Some of those radio waves carry a very negative message of warped sexuality, or rage and anger, or foolish arrogance—pick your poison—and some of those radio waves carry very positive messages like, "Straight from the Heart with Pastor Thom O'Leary!" Spiritual warfare is like the radio waves that carry negative messages. Any one of us can get some random, weird thought, and we even say to ourselves, "Where did *that* come from?!" Let me tell you where it came from... it came from the enemy of your soul. But know this—there is hope.

There Is Hope

Though there is a battle going on, you can be secure and stand in the face of attack. You can hold on and hang in there. You can weather the storms, because there is an anchor God offers you. I encourage you to memorize Hebrews 6:19,

> "We have this hope as an <u>anchor for the soul</u>, firm and secure."
> (NIV; underline added for emphasis)

Your hope in the Lord anchors down your soul. It keeps you steady. It makes you secure on the inside. The truth is this: no matter what happens in your life, place your hope in the Lord and let it be settled in the God who loves you and has your life in the palm of His hands. If you are feeling unsteady, or insecure, return to that hope.

Though there is a battle going on, you can be secure and stand in the face of attack.

So let's re-cap. We are getting ourselves ready to hear God's will and preparing our heart, mind, and soul. Your heart is your spiritual core; your mind is your thought life; your soul is your emotional well-being.

Finally in getting ready to know God's will for your life, Jesus said, "Love God with all your strength." Let's complete the preparation process to knowing God's will in the next chapter.

Factor One: The YOU Factor
Getting Ready
Fifth Preparation: Your Strength

Chapter 5
Assessing Your Strength

"I can do everything through him who gives me strength."
Philippians 4:13 (NIV)

I was lifting weights at a gym with a buddy of mine. One day we were feeling quite confident and began to load more and more weight on the barbell. It was my friend's turn to do his squats. He bent down, yet didn't come back up. I'm just casually watching him as his face began to turn red, while his knees were bent and legs were shaking. He attempted to mumble out some words, and I couldn't understand what in the world he was saying. I said,

"Excuse me?" He blurted out, "It ain't happening, bro'!" It finally dawned on me that he was stuck and out of strength! I immediately helped him up and took the weight off his shoulders. We didn't assess our strength very well in the gym that day, based on the weight we were putting on our shoulders.

There are times in life when we are carrying way too much weight on our shoulders and to be mumbling out the words, excuse the slang, "It ain't happening, bro'!" as if to say, "I'm not making it." If you are carrying too much weight on your shoulders, it will be horribly difficult to discern God's will for your life. You will have to unload your burdens and get rid of the unneeded weight that is bogging you down.

Habits, Hurts, and Hang-ups

What are the things that have you bogged down? Usually it comes down to three areas: *habits, hurts,* and *hang-ups.* I don't know if you have ever have gone to a garbage dump and unloaded junk from the back of a truck. It is an amazing feeling of getting rid of your junk, unloading your unwanted stuff, and living free and lighter. It is even more amazing to unload the junk of your personal life, where you sense God's peace and feel His nearness. That will lead you to a good place to hear from God and His will for your life—

which will require unloading your habits, hurts, and hang-ups.

If you are carrying too much weight on your shoulders, it will be horribly difficult to discern God's will for your life. You will have to unload your burdens and get rid of the unneeded weight that is bogging you down.

Unloading Your Habits

You may have formed *habits* that are not healthy. It could be too much or too little of certain things. Eating and drinking too much, or not getting enough sleep and exercise will sap your strength. Remember, getting ready to know God's will means becoming healthy in *all* areas of life.

It's time to get rid of those habits that are taking you away from God's will. Perhaps you have heard of the statement, "A thought can lead to an action, an action can lead to a habit, a habit can lead to a life, and a life leads us to eternity." If you are struggling with habits that are stealing your time, energy, and even money, go back to the thought that is initiating that action. Begin to unload those thoughts to God. You may need a trusted friend, or keen counselor, to share with. But as you get rid of negative habits, you will be preparing yourself to know God's will for your life.

Unloading Your Hurts

You may be carrying *hurts*. If the wrongs you've done or the wrongs done to you are heavy in your heart, you will be trudging along in life, like trying to run with ten-pound ankle weights.

When I was in high school running sprints on the football team, I had five-pound ankle weights on each leg. The coach yelled at me, "O'Leary, why are you running so slow?!" I was a pretty quick athlete back in the day, and the coach noticed something was wrong. I yelled back, "I got ankle weights on coach!" He shouted back, "Take them off so I can see what you can do!"

Unloading our hurts is like taking off ankle weights—so that we can run the race that we are designed for. Hebrews 12:1 says,

> "Therefore, since we are surrounded by such a great cloud of witnesses, let us throw off everything that hinders and the sin that so easily entangles. And let us run with

perseverance the race <u>marked out for us</u>."
(NIV; underline added for emphasis)

There is a race marked out specifically for you! But notice that we have to unload the weight—throw off anything that is hindering us from successfully running our race. That race marked out for you is God's will for your life.

Unloading Your Hang-ups

Hang-ups are those things that consume us and distract us. It could be little pet peeves that you are carrying that are taking way too much of your time. There comes a time in life where we have to just move on. Perhaps there are people in your life who have hurt you, and you continue to think about it all the time. The best thing you can do is to hand those people over to God, which means you are not going to carry that weight anymore. Doing that does not justify the wrongs they have done; in fact it makes them accountable to God. The best thing you could do is "let it go."

> ...getting ready to know God's will means becoming healthy in *all* areas of life.

Assessing your strength means getting rid of the habits, hurts, and hang-ups that are holding you back. It also means understanding where strength can be found.

> There is a race marked out specifically for you! ...
> That race marked out for you is God's will for your life.

Strength through Serving

Not only is it vital to get rid of unneeded weight on your shoulders, it is equally important to understand what can give you strength, where you are feeling strong in every area of life, where you are spiritually renewed, emotionally healthy, and physically refreshed. Assessing our strength is critical in knowing God's will for our lives—it's part of getting ready and being prepared to hear from God.

Believe it or not, strength is found when we serve others. Jesus gave us an incredible life-altering principle when he said, "Give, and you will receive." When we serve others, something happens to us! As we make a difference in someone's life, we in return get energized.

Assessing your strength is understanding that it is a process that calls people to service, revealing how we gain

God's strength when we serve others. As you serve other people, God begins revealing His plan for you. It's all part of the process of knowing what God has for you, knowing His will. It begins with an attitude of service.

> ...strength is found when we serve others.

An Attitude of Service: First One On the Field and Last One Off

In the movie *We Were Soldiers*, Mel Gibson plays the real life of Hal Moore, a military colonel. One of his life principles was to be the first man on the battlefield and the last one off, demonstrating a life of dedication, preparation, and strength. There is a vivid picture in my mind from the movie, where the colonel's boot is lifting off the ground as he steps into the helicopter, as the last one off the battlefield.

From my football days to being a Lead Pastor, I have taken that attitude, and have attempted to be the first one on and the last one off! As an athlete I made it a "game" to be the first one on the field and the last one off. I would be out on the field warming up when other guys would begin to show up. And I would do sprints or drills until I saw the last player walk off the field. Only then could I hit the showers! As a Lead Pastor, I have tried to model service and sacrifice to those around me, whether it's picking up trash while walking across our church campus, or being prepared for a meeting.

Being the "first one on and last one off" in life means sacrifice, preferring others, and serving others. It really is a state of mind or attitude.

We find incredible strength in God, when we serve others for His sake. Jesus said to love God with all our heart, mind, soul, and strength. Loving God with our strength is service on his behalf. It is making a difference in the lives of others. When we are looking to make a difference in the lives of others by serving them, that attitude gets us ready to know His will for our lives. Strength and service go hand in hand. Yet, we have to make sure that we are serving out of healthy place. After all, our strength is found in Him.

Our strength is found in Him.

Searching for Strength in God

There is a strength that we find when we search for God and His will for our lives, as it says in Psalm 105:4,

> "Search for the LORD and for His strength,
> and keep on searching." (NLT)

We search for God by praying and meditating. We search for God by reading scripture. We search for God by worshipping Him with others. The "search" never stops— we are to keep on searching.

To discover God's will, you have to passionately go after God. Search means be intentional and go after His strength. And whatever you do, don't quit searching!

When my kids were small, we would play "hide and seek." I would find a great hiding place, taking the game very seriously, of course. The problem would be that every so often they would get distracted. Twenty minutes later I would come out of hiding and they would be playing a new game, having totally forgotten about me and our game of "hide and seek"! Sometimes we can get distracted in life and forget about the search for God.

Avoiding Sapping Distractions

Distractions are all around us. They're different for everyone. Some people are distracted by drowning themselves at work, while others are caught up in so much recreation that God has been placed on the back burner. It's crazy to think that the average American watches eight hours of television per day! With sleep and work, it's hard to imagine that someone could be watching that much TV. Hours upon hours can be wasted when God is waiting to do something great in your life.

To help avoid distractions, don't quit searching and seeking. If you keep searching, you will find Him. Remember, God loves to play hide and seek! Not that He is trying to hide from you. However, <u>He loves it when you seek Him</u>.

Whatever you do, you should being doing it from the strength God provides, as it says in 1 Peter 4:11,

> "If anyone serves, he should <u>do it with the strength God provides</u>, so that in all things God may be praised through Jesus Christ." (NIV; underline added for emphasis)

Serving God means you are engaged in ministry, and you serve other people. The key to preventing burnout is serving out of the grace and strength He provides, instead of out of your own strength. This is all a part of discovering God's will for your life. As you serve others, God begins revealing what He has for you. It's all a part of the process.

> Remember, God loves to play hide and seek! Not that He is trying to hide from you.
> However, <u>He loves it when you seek Him</u>.

Two Dimensions of the Grace of God

Never forget Philippians 4:13,

> "I can do everything through Him who gives me strength." (NIV)

You can do anything and everything you need to, through the help and strength of Christ. And that's called the grace of God. God's grace has two dimensions. One dimension is *His unmerited favor and free gift of salvation.* Another dimension is to *give you the power to do what He calls you to do.* 'Truth be known, He will give you the grace to know His will and to do His will.

You need to absolutely know that you know that God loves you. And it is true that He has a plan for your life. So as you love God with all your heart, all your mind, all your soul, and all your strength, you are setting yourself up to know His will for your life!

This renewing on the inside of your heart, mind, soul and strength is where it all begins. My friend, Scott Underwood wrote a popular worship song titled, "Take My Life" where the lyrics go,

> *Take my heart and form it, Take my mind, transform it, Take my will, conform it, to Yours, to Yours, Oh Lord.*

That is exactly what we are talking about in Getting Ready... getting yourself in a good place with God to hear His will—that's **The YOU Factor!** It means getting you ready and preparing yourself to receive God's will.

Now that there is an understanding of Factor One: **The YOU Factor**, getting ready to hear from God, let's recap:

Factor One: The YOU Factor—Getting Ready
First Preparation: Understanding God's Will
Second Preparation: Your Heart
Third Preparation: Your Mind
Fourth Preparation: Your Soul
Fifth Preparation: Your Strength

By God's grace, let's move on to Factor Two: **The GOD Factor!**

Factor Two: The GOD Factor
Five Ways God Speaks to Us
First Way

"God does speak — now one way, now another — though no one perceives it." Job 33:14 (NIV)

Chapter 6
His Word

"For the word of God is living and active."
Hebrews 4:12 (NIV)

A doctor tells the story of checking in a new patient, a little boy, into a hospital room. The doctor forgot to tell the boy how the intercom worked. The little boy all alone in the room, pushed the call button and the doctor said over the intercom, *"Yes, Billy what do you need?"* There was complete silence, so he repeated himself, *"Billy, what do you need?"* Billy blurts out, *"I hear you God, but I can't see you!"*

Sadly many people are *not* seeing God, but even more tragic, they are *not* hearing God, either. We have to be able to see His handiwork and hear His voice to discover His will. God is always speaking. He is whispering to our souls, nudging our hearts, and giving us loud wake-up calls, though most people, tragically, miss what God is saying.

God sometimes speaks to us in one way and then sometimes He will speak to us in a whole different method. Yet, ultimately He is trying to get our attention! When I look back at my life and how God has navigated me through situations and circumstances, I cannot imagine where I would be without God's guiding voice. The key is intentionally listening for His voice.

The starting point for God speaking to us is that He speaks primarily through His Word, the Bible, and all the other ways that He speaks to us that are discussed in this book are in light of God's Word. That means the only reason we know that God speaks to us in other ways is that the Bible tells us so. When hearing from God, the message must never contradict God's Word. God would never contradict Himself. So everything must always line up with His written Word. If you think that God is saying to you,

"I should hate my neighbor" that would be a wrong answer! In the words of a football referee, that would be a *"Penalty, 15 yards, Personal Infraction!"* God would never contradict Himself, and His Word already tells us to love our neighbor as our self. (Note to self: The Golden Rule!)

However, there are some essential truths that scripture speaks of that are very helpful for us to discover God's will. Let's examine what His Word tells us.

God Is Always Speaking

If you want to know God's will, the good news is, God does speak. In fact, God is always speaking. Throughout history God has always communicated with His people and continues to communicate to His people. He is the same yesterday, today and forever. He does not change like shifting shadows. God is always speaking.

God Speaks in Different Ways

Scripture tells us that God speaks in different ways. That is important to understand. It's like a friend of yours who can choose to communicate with you in many different ways. Your friend could choose to call you on a cell phone, or talk to you face to face, text you, email you, send a card in the mail, or even use social media to reach you! It's their choice how they want to communicate with you. So it is with the Lord. It's His choice how He wants to communicate with you. We can't put God in a box and say that He only speaks *one* way, because that would go against what His Word has already told us.

People Do Not Always Understand

We are going to work on that! Coming to know God's will for your life means understanding how God might reveal His will to *you*. The fact that *"people do not always understand"* is a great warning to us to *not* be those types of people! This is a wake-up call to be alert, to apply ourselves to understanding how God speaks.

Given that God does speak in so many different ways, we need to understand what He is saying. A great example of this is found in the story of Elijah in the Old Testament and the lesson that he had to learn. Elijah is on top of a mountain and the Lord is going to pass in front of him. A wind comes blasting through, shattering rocks in its path. After the wind, an earthquake rumbles across the mountain range which I'm sure left Elijah shaking in his boots, or sandals, whatever the case may be. After the earthquake, fire blasts in front of Elijah, and then there is a still small voice. Elijah learns that the Lord was not in the wind, was not in the earthquake, and was not in the fire. God simply spoke in a still small voice.

God does not always speak in a sonic boom, or thundering voice, *"Let there be Light!"* If we get distracted, busy, or are looking in the wrong places, we can miss His still small voice. We can be looking for the big dramatic moment to know God's will and He is in the whisper of life. God wants to have a relationship with us and relationship always means communication—God wants to guide our lives, and will as we listen to Him.

We can be looking for the big dramatic moment to know
God's will and
He is in the whisper of life.

That is the wonderful thing about God's Word, the Bible. It is always there, and is always available. You can pick it up over and over again. It is always speaking and always ready to guide us. It is the guiding force of truth. It is the plumb line to which we can line up our lives. I was told by a friend of mine who is in construction that a plumb line is a simple but accurate tool that is used to determine if something is perfectly vertical. God's Word perfectly aligns us vertically to God's will.

He's given us His word as the ultimate yardstick and everything needs to be measured by His Word. We certainly can't measure perfection by setting ourselves as models of perfection... it's simply not possible. But even though we will never be perfect, God's Word is perfect. As we look at the other ways God speaks to us, always keep in mind that those ways always need to line up to the perfect plumb line and be measured by the ultimate yardstick, the authority of the Bible.

When someone discovers that the Holy Spirit will speak through the written Word and lead them to the truth—look out—life becomes a whole new world! It's like walking into a dark room, flicking on the light switch and *boom*, what couldn't be seen now can be seen. How that practically works is by reading God's Word and the Holy Spirit will begin to illuminate what is being read. He will begin to give you answers that are hidden within the pages.

Jesus said it this way...

> "But when he, the Spirit of truth, comes, <u>he will guide you</u> into all truth. He will not speak on his own; <u>he will speak</u> only what he hears,

and <u>he will tell you</u> what is yet to come."
John 16:13
(NIV; underlines added for emphasis)

Jesus was simply saying that after He physically would leave earth that the Holy Spirit would guide your life. That is a very simple concept and yet incredibly powerful. If you've got big decisions to make, know that God wants to help you and guide you, through His Word.

Sometimes we need to be taught, and sometimes we need to be rebuked. At other moments we need to be corrected, and sometimes we simply need to be trained. That makes me think of a child in an elementary class. The child needs to be taught the lesson, but if he is jumping up and down on his desk and pouring milk over the head of the little girl who is sitting next to him—he needs a rebuke! If the child is talking during the class when he is not supposed to, then he needs to be corrected. Ultimately, the teacher needs to train the child, and the child also needs to listen and choose to change his behavior!

We are God's children and God's Word has the power to teach us, rebuke us, correct us, and train us. Ultimately, it's His Word that shapes us and gets us on the right path.

As 2 Timothy 3:16-17 says,

> "¹⁶<u>All Scripture is God-breathed</u> and is useful for teaching, rebuking, correcting and training in righteousness, ¹⁷ so that the people of God may be thoroughly equipped for every good work."
> (NIV; underline added for emphasis)

All scripture is from the breath of God. He breathed it into certain people to write it down, so we could get to know Him. Many people wrestle with the question, *"Could there be human error?"* Let's look at Hebrews 6:18 and then let's answer some questions.

> "So God has given us both his promise and his oath. These two things are unchangeable because <u>it is impossible for God to lie</u>. Therefore, we who have fled to him for refuge can take new courage, for we can hold on to his promise with confidence."
> (NLT; underline added for emphasis)

Four Primary Ways Why We Can Fully Trust God's Word

God has given us a promise and an oath, which were written down, so that they could be passed on through the centuries. Therefore, there are four primary ways *why we can fully trust God's Word—the Bible*:

1. *Did Jesus believe the Old Testament was the Word of God?* Jesus believed and quoted the Old Testament Scripture. If someone believed that Jesus was of God then they would have to embrace what He confirmed. It brings a person to ask and decide, "Was Jesus right or wrong?" "Do I agree or disagree with Him?" Jesus confirmed the authority of the Old Testament.

2. *Who actually wrote the New Testament?* Only Apostles who encountered Jesus wrote the New Testament letters. Jesus confirmed the Old Testament, and those whose lives were transformed by Christ wrote the New Testament. And all of the Apostles have complete unity in their message. It would be like ten people witnessing a car accident and each were asked to write a report of the crash for the police, and all ten reports had the exact same description... the exact same message.

3. *Is the scripture we read the same that was originally written?* The scripture we read is the scripture the first church read. We are not playing the "telephone game"! The telephone game is the game where one person whispers something in someone's ear, and they whisper to the next person what they thought they heard, and it goes around the circle with the last person blurting out what they heard—it's usually not even close to what was originally said. The discovery of the Dead Sea Scrolls in the 1950's put an end to this debate. The scripture we read is the scripture the first churches were reading.

4. *Is the Bible reliable?* Holy Scripture has been used by the Christian community for nearly 2,000 years and it works... it changes lives! Here's the deal, the proof of the pudding is in the eating! Try reading it and it will come alive in your life. God's written Word is always there for us and is our manual for living. Anytime you are going through something where you need an answer, the first thing you should do is say, *"Huh, I wonder what the Bible has to say about that?"*

Maybe you have questions about finances. The Bible talks about money almost more than any other topic. Perhaps you have questions about your marriage. The Bible speaks about marriage and gives solid answers. How about questions about sex? The Bible even talks about sex!

One thing I have discovered is that the more emotionally tied we are to a decision we need to make while searching for God's will, the more difficult it can be to discern His will. That's another great reason why His Word comes in handy!

Hebrews 4:12 says,

> "The Word of God is living and active. Sharper than any double-edged sword, it penetrates even to dividing soul and spirit, joints and marrow; it judges the thoughts and attitudes of the heart." (NIV)

Our soul is more on the emotional side of our beings. This is reminding us that God's Word can separate our emotions and our spirit with laser beam accuracy.

God can reveal His will for you through His Word. Yet, as Job 33:14 tells us, God speaks in different ways. Yet all those ways must line up with His Word, the Bible.

God can reveal His will for you through His Word.

Let's continue our search and understanding of Factor Two: **The God Factor**—and the four other primary ways that God speaks to us. One of them is: God will inevitably speak to you through other people... whether you like it or not!

Factor Two: The GOD Factor
Five Ways God Speaks to Us
Second Way

Chapter 7
Through Other People

"...words taught by the Spirit..."
1 Corinthians 2:13 (NIV)

When searching for God's will for our lives, we have to be open to the ways that God will bring forth His plan. This is what I know, that God will use certain people in our lives to reveal His will. It could be a parent. It could be a close friend. It might even be a pastor! In the Old Testament God used a donkey to speak to a fellow named Balaam. So my thought is, *"If God could use a donkey, He could use me!"*

How a Human Being Can Speak the Words of God

There was a time in my life when I was searching for an answer. A friend walked by me and said, "I believe the Lord wants you to know that He is calling you to the 'hill'. Not to the 'mountain', but rather to the 'hill.'" My church is named Mountainbrook Community Church, so he was making sure I knew what he was talking about. Now that message of "going to the hill" would not have any meaning to most people, however it spoke volumes to me, and answered my prayer that I was asking the Lord. God uses people to speak to us His will.

I love how the Bible describes how a human being can speak the words of God to someone.

1 Corinthians 2:13 says,

> "We do not use words that come from human wisdom. Instead, we speak <u>words given to us by the Spirit</u>, using the Spirit's words to explain spiritual truths."
> (NLT; underline added for emphasis)

God will speak through pastors and gifted Bible teachers as they explain spiritual truths. I can't tell you how many times I have given a message and someone says to me,

"How'd you know that was going on in my life?!" Or better yet, someone will say to me, "You were preaching just to me!" I typically will respond jokingly with, "Yes, I've been breaking into your house and reading your mail!"

The truth is, God speaks through His Word and His Spirit in very specific and accurate ways. How could someone think that an entire message (sermon) was just for them and not for the other 99 or 999 or 9,999 people listening? That's the Lord revealing His will in a wonderfully personal way. Based on that reality, it's important to go to church worship services so that you are placing yourself in a good position to be spoken to. It's like the fisherman—drop your hook where the fish are biting!

There is an awesome phenomenon of preaching and teaching God's Word, and the way God speaks into lives. Before I speak at my church on a Sunday morning, I say a simple prayer that goes something like this, "God, thank You for the power of Your Word and thank You for the power of Your Holy Spirit. Speak to us now through Your Word and by Your Spirit."

Prophetic Messages

The Bible talks about people speaking into other people's lives through "prophetic" messages. Now trust me, not all "prophetic" words are from God. I am reminded of some prophetic bloopers. There was an elderly British woman that cried out to a crowd (say this sentence in a voice of a Monty Python spoof of an elderly British woman), "God would say... God would say... well, first of all, God would say, 'Merry Christmas!'" Or the person that tried to use King James language, "Yay, you have heard of the atomic bomb... yay, you have heard of the nuclear bomb... but I now give you the balm of Gilead!" I think this lady had her "bombs" mixed up! Or finally, the man who said to a group speaking for God, "I know you are tired and discouraged. I get that way sometimes." Let me assure you that God never gets tired and is never emotionally discouraged! Perhaps, disappointed at the decisions of human beings—but never discouraged!

You have heard children say the "darnedest things" yet adults will say even more of the "darnedest things." Even though there are a lot of things said by people with God's nametag on it that are wacko, *don't throw the baby out with the bath water!*

God will use people to shape your life and lead you to His will for your life. As one of my mentors used to say, "Eat the meat and throw out the bones."

The Bible talks about a prophetic message that can be given through mature leaders.

1 Timothy 4:14 reminds us,

> "Do not neglect your gift, which was given you through a <u>prophetic message</u> when the body of elders laid their hands on you."
> (NIV; underline added for emphasis)

A Prophetic Message Has Two Elements: Forth-Telling and Foretelling

When I was attending seminary, I was given really helpful insight into what prophecy is and how it works. A prophetic message has two elements. One element is *forth-telling* which means it is a message of righteousness and honesty, declaring what God says is good, right, and true. Typically, it can be convicting, confronting, or en-couraging—but never should it bring condemnation.

There is a difference between condemnation and conviction. Condemnation beats a person down, tells them they are worthless, and basically the scum of the earth! No, worse than that, it tells them they are the scum on the bottom of a scum pond!! No, even worse than that, it tells them they are the scum that eats the scum on the bottom of a scum pond!!! Okay, you get the point. Condemnation destroys a person and attempts to blast them into smithereens.

Conviction, on the other hand, is different from condemnation. Conviction can be confrontational, and even expose what is wrong in a person's life, yet its purpose is to correct, shape, and mold someone for the better. Conviction is what God uses. Condemnation is what the devil uses. Conviction brings about the necessary truth to change what is wrong. It's like a coach who instructs his or her athlete that how they are performing is not bringing the greatest results and if they change what they are doing—it will enhance their performance greatly. This way is similar to conviction, versus the coach that just stands there and shouts at the player, "You stink!"

So the first element of a prophetic message is forth-telling, that is telling the truth. The second element of a prophetic message is *foretelling*, which is understood to relay to people "what is to come."

One of the best examples in the Bible of foretelling is the story of Jonah. Jonah was given a message from God for the city of Nineveh. The simple message that he was to deliver to the people was, "Stop acting evil!" That part of the message was really forth-telling. This is the idea of speaking righteousness. The second part of the message went something like this, "If you don't, bad things are going to happen." That part of the message would be considered foretelling, that is, telling what will happen in the future by God's decision.

God used a man named Jonah to speak to the people of Nineveh. Once Jonah got up the nerve to actually deliver the message, the people listened and surprisingly they repented and were blessed to not live through the consequences of their evil practices. The bottom line is that they got the message of God's will for their life and welcomed it gladly.

This is not just a fun story in the Bible; it is a story of God speaking through a person to bring about His will. Today, in the 21st Century, God still uses people to reveal His will to other people.

There was a person who I don't even know well that helped me understand God's will on a matter that I was searching out. I had felt like God was speaking to me to change the name of our church. If you have been in any church, you know that changing the church's name is tampering with the "holy grail." I was not just going on a whim, or pulling the "thus saith the Lord" card. I really wanted to be patient and truly know that I was hearing from God and discerning His perfect will as it related to the changing of our church's name.

I was heading for a conference, and God had strongly impressed on me to talk with a particular pastor. I only knew his name, as we briefly met just once before. I didn't even necessarily know that he would be at this event that was out of state for both of us. So I simply prayed, "God if it is truly your will that I speak to this man, then make it happen."

My wife and I fly into this major U.S. city for the conference and go to lunch. Now, you may not believe this, but out of the thousands of places to go eat lunch, in a city of a million plus, this pastor is eating lunch at the same restaurant! I whisper to my wife, "That's the guy I'm supposed to talk to." She said with all wisdom and encouragement, "Well, then, go over and talk to him." I totally chickened out and said, "No, he's with his family, I don't want to bother him." (That was partly true, because as a pastor in a medium-sized community, people stop me frequently. However, truth be known, I think I was being a "scaredy-cat!") So I prayed again, "Lord if you really want me to speak with this pastor – then set it up one more time." This was a bit of a "Gideon move," throwing my fleece out for a second time. (Refer to Judges 6:36-40 in the Old Testament of the Bible!)

I went to the first session of the conference. When it had finished I walked out a side door and there before me was this pastor that I felt I was suppose to talk to. He was sitting on a bench all by himself, almost looking like he was waiting for someone. I looked to Heaven and said to God, "Okay, okay, I'll talk to him!"

I went up to him and introduced myself, reconnecting to the first time we met. We stood there talking about church life... attendance, small groups, buildings—the kind of stuff that bores most people and perks the ears of every pastor. We talked for about fifteen minutes and were at that point where you could feel the conversation was dwindling to an end. I began to shake his hand, still not knowing why I had felt God wanted me to talk to him. As I said good-bye, I stopped in a quick moment and spontaneously asked, "By the way, what's the name of your church?" He told me that he just changed the name of his church, and the name change was almost exactly the change of name that I sensed God was having us make.

After he told me his story of changing his church name, I shared with him what I felt God was calling us to do with changing the name of our church. He looked straight into my eyes and said, "That's totally God." We finally said our "good-byes" and I walked away with God's nudge in my heart, "That's why you needed to talk to him." I haven't ever seen him since, though it was evident to me that God spoke through a person to reveal His ultimate will for the very thing I was praying for.

Not Everything That People Say with the Tag of God's Name Is Truly from God

Let's be clear here, not everything that people say with the tag of God's name is truly from God. And later we will take a strong, in-depth look at how to test a "so-called" word from God—that's Factor Four of our Five Factors. Yet, be open to God using other people in your life to reveal His will. It's one of the five major ways that He speaks to us.

Factor One is **The YOU Factor**, getting yourself ready to hear from God. This is where we prepare our heart, mind, soul, and strength to hear from God. Factor Two is **The GOD Factor**, specifically discovering the five major ways that God speaks to us. We began with God's Word, which is supreme to the other four major ways and where every other way must line up. We now should understand that God will use people in our lives to speak His plan for us, from a pastor giving a message to a totally random person.

Now we go to the third major way where God can reveal His will for our lives. In the words of a surgeon, "Hand me a scalpel," as we are going to have to cut deep within. God has the awesome ability to bring conviction and impressions to the depth and core of who we are.

Factor Two: The GOD Factor
Five Ways God Speaks to Us
Third Way

Chapter 8
Via Conviction and Impressions

"...with power, with the Holy Spirit and with deep conviction..."
1 Thessalonians 1:5 (NIV)

Do you ever wonder why God doesn't just yell your name, "Hey, Bob, wrong move, don't go there!" Or, "Hey, Suzy, you'll want to double check that one!" You know what I mean, where God would just call your name and in an audible voice say it plainly.

When I was in high school I worked on a chicken farm. If you saw the movie *Napoleon Dynamite*, it was exactly like that chicken farm! Even the chicken farm owner I worked for looked frighteningly the same as the one in the movie. I would push these carts down long aisles, bird feathers everywhere, bird poop everywhere, and chickens squawking at the top of their lungs. (Chickens have lungs, right?) After a while, you started to think the chickens were calling your name. They would screech, "Bock, bock, bock, ba-Thom, ba-Thom!" It freaked me out. What if God called your name out of the blue? It would probably freak you out. Well, God is always speaking, through His word and through His Spirit, and prompting us via conviction and impressions.

Conviction and Impressions—When God Does Something on the Inside that Reveals His Will

"Conviction and impressions" are experienced when God does something on the inside of us that reveals His will. He does not use words alone, but many times uses deep conviction that grabs a hold of your gut. If a person is trying to discover God's will and is experiencing deep conviction, that is probably God speaking to them.

Scripture says in 1 Thessalonians 1:5,

> "...our gospel came to you <u>not simply with words</u>, but also with power, with the Holy Spirit and with <u>deep conviction</u>."
> (NIV; underlines added for emphasis)

God was revealing His will not just through words, but rather with deep conviction by His Spirit. If you are trying to discover God's will and you are experiencing deep conviction, it is highly probable that God is speaking to you to do what's right.

In John 14:26, Jesus says,

> "The Holy Spirit... will be your teacher and will <u>bring to your mind</u> all I have said to you."
> (NIV; underline added for emphasis)

Jesus said part of the "job description" of the Holy Spirit is to bring things to your mind. The Holy Spirit will impress things on your mind. That is what is called an impression.

Perhaps you have felt burdened for someone out of the blue, so you call them and say, "You've been on my heart and I have sensed you were struggling." They respond in a shocked manner, "How did you know?!" When that happens, you were responding to an impression that God gave you.

I send out a weekly devotional by email called, "E-Heart to Heart" to thousands of people; however, my older brother is not one of those people on our database list. All of a sudden I feel "impressed" that I'm supposed to send this "E-Heart to Heart" to him that was based on Galatians 6:9 that talks about not quitting, yet doing good, and at the right time God will reward you. I forwarded the devotional to him and he emails me back, "Thom, I feel like quitting, I'm asking God are you there? Will you speak to me? And I get your email that says, 'Don't quit, God is speaking.'"

I responded to an impression that God was giving me, and that resulted in the Lord speaking to my brother. Be open to conviction and impressions, you never know what God might do!

We have to understand that God is always with us. One of His precious promises is, "I will never leave you." You can trust that. God wouldn't have said it—if it weren't true. God cannot lie. He wasn't thinking, "I'm going to fool them! I'll say, 'I'll never leave them' and then trick them and leave them!" No, God makes a promise to never leave you and because he will never leave you, that means He is here to help you, lead you, guide you. And He brings conviction and impressions into our lives to accomplish that.

God is like a parent who wants the best for his child, and will communicate difficult messages through conviction and impressions. A parent who loves their children or child desires deeply to communicate effectively with that child, even if the message is hard to hear. The parents, in love, will still communicate the message despite how difficult or awkward it will be, because they believe it will help the child. That's the loving thing to do.

In the same way, God will bring conviction to your life over the problem of sin, when we are missing the target. He will impress upon you the consequences of your decisions. Sin weighs you down, hinders you, entangles and ties you up from completing the purpose of your life!

Hebrews 12:1 reminds us,

> "Therefore, since we are surrounded by such a great cloud of witnesses, let us throw off everything that hinders and the sin that so easily entangles, and let us run with perseverance the race marked out for us." (NIV)

"A cloud of witnesses" are those who have gone before us, who have walked out the life God intended. With those people in mind, "let us throw off," that is to say, "strip away, cut loose the extra-baggage!"

God uses conviction and impressions in your life so that you can get rid of the extra weight that sin causes. When you respond to that type of conviction, you will run light and free, and be able to do what you were made to do.

Fix Your Eyes on the One Who Can Write Your Life Story

Another frequent impression that will lead you to God's will for your life can come when you fix your eyes on the one who can write your life story. The Lord is the author of your destiny. He is the one that shapes it and is the finisher of it.

In a relay race, whether it is track, swimming, or another sporting event, typically the strongest or fastest goes last to bring completion to the race. That's what the Lord does; He brings completion to your life. Follow His conviction and impressions. Because He's the finisher, He'll take you to the finish line—His will for your life!

> Because He's the finisher, He'll take you to the finish line—His will for your life!

Another key insight to grasp is that God's conviction and impressions are seriously for our good, because they are motivated by love!

I love how honest scripture is when it says, in Hebrews 12:11,

"No discipline seems pleasant at the time— but painful!" (NIV)

But it produces really good things in our lives, like righteousness and peace, for those who are "trained" by it. If you are going to go through discipline, it would be wise to be trained by it. That means learn from it!

A parent who really loves his or her child will try their best to train and correct their child so that they will learn life and will gain wisdom. A great definition of wisdom is "skill for life." God wants us to have wisdom—skill for life—so He gives us conviction and impressions!

Following God's conviction and impressions are literally steps to the finish line. However, discovering God's will for your life is not a sprint—it's a marathon. I read an article about a guy who ran in the New York City Marathon. He said the first half of that race is a party. Apparently in the beginning you are swept along by 28,000 runners, crowds lining the streets, and people running in costumes. Then you find yourself touring the ethnic neighborhoods of Brooklyn and Queens. In this moment he said that you feel like you could run forever. When runners hit mile 13, they cross over into Manhattan and start heading north, away from the finish line. At this point Central Park is behind you, and runners are now moving in the wrong direction for the finish line! The author of the article confesses that the crowds are thinner now—the party's over.

His experience continued where between mile 16 and 18, the runners hit the wall. This is the moment where they are absolutely miserable. They are physically and psychologically busted. Everything inside is screaming to stop running. As this runner passed one of the first aid stations there were runners lying on cots, looking "pale and gaunt," with IV's dripping into their arms. He thought to himself, "Those lucky dogs!" This was the point of despair. He imagined himself having to go home and tell everybody he didn't finish. He was thinking, "Why did I ever sign up for this race? What made me think I could do this?"

He then realized that one way or another, he had to get to Central Park. That's where his ride was. He had no car. He had no money. He would have to get there on his own two feet. So he might as well keep running, just putting one foot in front of the other. He didn't want to think about the next 6 miles; just think about the next step. He knew if he could keep that up, keep putting one foot in front of the other, the miles would pass. He made it and testified that when you cross that finish line, it feels like glory—even if you're in 10,044[th] place!

Discovering God's will for your life is not a sprint—
it's a marathon.

Some of you reading this book may be hitting the wall right now, feeling like you can't go on, like you'll never make it. Following God's conviction and impressions perhaps is harder than you ever imagined it would be, and you're thinking about giving up, about doing something foolish. Don't do it!

There's no magic to endurance racing. It's all about continuing and following one step after another. Following God's conviction and impressions are steps to the finish line.

Striving for Peace

God's conviction and impressions should ultimately produce peace in your life, or lead you to peace. There is a power in striving for peace, contending for peace, even with your enemies, and it leads to what God wants to do in your life.

Hebrews 12:14 calls us to,

> "Make every effort to live in peace with all
> people and to be holy; without holiness no one
> will see the Lord." (NIV)

We are called to not just make peace with some people, but *all* people! When we follow this conviction, it leads you to being holy. Then we can see that holiness is so important to see God working in your life. Holy means "set apart for God."

Striving for peace places you on the mature road. It's easy to blow people off! It's easy to hate someone. But following God's conviction and impressions to strive for peace is making every effort you can, and then, trusting God. Yet we have to do our part.

Dealing with Bitterness

Another conviction and impression that God will give so that you can know His will for your life is on the subject of bitterness. Bitterness is like a cancer that will eat you from the inside out.

Hebrews 12:15 says,

> "See to it that no one misses the grace of God and that no bitter root grows up to cause trouble and defile many." (NIV)

There are three things that bitterness causes. It makes you "miss God's grace," it causes "deep trouble in your life," and then it "defiles others." That word *defile* means, "taint" or "corrupt" or "pollute." Your bitterness taints other people and the plan of evil loves it. Bitterness gets people frustrated, fragmented, and ultimately missing God's will for their life.

Many people think, "I have a right to be bitter!" Well maybe they do, and maybe not. But the bottom line is bitterness is destroying their life, and their bitterness doesn't get back at the other person. In fact, it's ruining them and those around them. Follow God's conviction and impressions to let go of bitterness.

Warning Signs

Via conviction and impressions, God gives warning signs. Recently I got a warning sign while driving my car. I was backing up in a parking lot and suddenly out of the side of my vision—my peripheral vision—I see a car heading toward me. We almost crashed, only to find out that it was my wife backing up in the same parking lot. Wouldn't *that* have been an insurance bummer? The insurance company would ask, "Whose fault is it?" I would probably respond with, "Mine, hers, I don't know which one costs less?!"

Now here's the deal, God gives warning signs via conviction and impressions. Through that near miss God gave me the impression of something much deeper than a fender-bender. He impressed on me, "Use caution, don't hurt family, and don't back into them. You're on the same team!"

Let me give you a challenge: be open to the tugs of the heart, the Holy Spirit nudges, that feeling in your gut, because God can speak to you through conviction and impressions. Being awake to God speaking to us is so key to knowing His will. But did you know that God can speak to you while you're sleeping? We will now dive deep into dreams and visions, the fourth major way that God speaks... because dreams do come true!

Factor Two: The GOD Factor
Five Ways God Speaks to Us
Fourth Way

Chapter 9
In Dreams and Visions

*"He speaks in dreams, in visions of the night, when deep
sleep falls on people as they lie in their beds."*
Job 33:15 (NLT)

In His word, God tells us that visions and dreams are
alive and active. Not every dream is from God, yet this
chapter gives a guide and understanding of how God uses
dreams.

Look at how the Bible explains this in Job 33:15-16,

> "God <u>speaks in dreams</u>, in <u>visions</u> of the
> night, when deep sleep falls on people lie in
> their beds. He <u>whispers in their ears</u>."
> (NLT; underlines added for emphasis)

Notice that God is speaking over and over again. However, is every dream that you have from God? *No!* Your thoughts, your fears, can influence dreams you are having. The Bible speaks of spiritual warfare in Ephesians Chapter 6 that potentially could affect the thoughts you are having, thus the dreams that you have. Some dreams are plain weird because you had too much food the night before! Those are what I call "Pizza Dreams."

However, the reality is there are times that God uses dreams to speak to people. Acts 2:17 reminds us,

> "In the last days, God says, 'I will pour out
> my Spirit on all people. Your sons and
> daughters will prophesy, your young men will
> see visions, your old men will dream dreams.'"
> (NIV)

In His word, God tells us that visions and dreams will be alive and active in the last days; they were not just used in

Biblical times. And what is so interesting is that I have read this verse a million times, and the light bulb went on when I read it for the millionth-and-one time! God will pour out His spirit "on all people." That means anybody can come to God, get to know Him through Christ, and God will reveal His will to them. Everyone is invited to hear from God, as He desires to pour out His Spirit on all people. And when that happens, people start having dreams and visions that are from God.

In His word, God tells us that visions and dreams will be alive and active in the last days;
they were not just used in Biblical times.

Is Every Dream Literal?

Sometimes a dream from God isn't literal, but is used as a warning. Years ago when I was a College Pastor, I had taken a large group of college students on a trip through western states, doing outreach and ministry on college campuses. We called our great adventure, "How the West was Won!"

While traveling through Colorado, we were given the opportunity to have a retreat in the mountains at a remote cabin. The night before we are to leave for the retreat, my wife has a dream that one of our vans that we were using tumbled off the cliff of a winding road while driving up to the cabin. It was a tragic dream; however, it was also a warning. That morning we gathered our team together, loaded up our two commercial vans, and then I had everyone huddle together, telling them I had something highly important to share with them. I explained how God uses dreams to warn us because he loves us. I then went on to explain the dream. I have never seen college students' eyes get so big! I calmly shared that we are going to pray for protection, drive very slow, and be completely cautious. So we prayed, slowly made our way to the cabin, and arrived unharmed. The road we drove was winding, with steep inclines covered with gravel, and huge drop-off cliffs. It could have been easy to drive carelessly, if we were not warned in a dream to be careful. The dream was a gracious warning from God.

Throughout the Bible God used dreams as warnings. Matthew 2:12 tells how God warned the Magi (Wise Men) who had come to worship and bring gifts to baby Jesus.

The passage explains,

"Having been <u>warned in a dream</u> not to go back to Herod, they returned back to their country by another route."

(NIV; underline added for emphasis)

We don't know what the dream was exactly, though it obviously communicated, somehow—someway, that King Herod was out to use the Magi to get to Jesus, because he desired to kill any potential kings. So the Wise Men took heed from the dream, altered their route, avoided King Herod, and protected the baby who was the Messiah. God's will was revealed through a dream!

Does God Speak Directly through a Dream?

God can do anything He wants; after all, He's God. So dreams can be very direct and informative. Speaking of the Magi and the Messiah, most people forget that even the name "Jesus" was revealed in a *dream*. As the story goes, Mary was with child through the Holy Spirit, or in other words, was pregnant and Joseph knew he wasn't the father! To say the least that news would be alarming to any young man, who was pledged to be married. Finding out that your fiancé is pregnant is not the type of news you want to hear! Joseph was such a good man that he did not want to publicly disgrace Mary, exposing her pregnancy that would have been devastating to her. Joseph thought of breaking off their marriage quietly, and I'm sure he was searching for God's will... His good, perfect and pleasing will.

Matthew 1:20-21 tells us that Joseph got his answer, God's will for his life, through a dream, a dream that would ultimately reveal the name of the Messiah.

The passage says,

> "But after he had considered this, an angel of the Lord appeared to him <u>in a dream</u> and said, 'Joseph son of David, do not be afraid to take Mary home as your wife, because what is conceived in her is from the Holy Spirit. She will give birth to a son, and you are to give him the name Jesus, because he will save his people from their sins." (NIV; underline for emphasis)

Joseph must have been an emotional wreck prior to that dream! Swirling within his heart; desperately searching for answers. And God meets him there, revealing His will through a dream. Joseph has this dream of an angel explaining everything. Most people think of the angel coming to Joseph in the physical world, however it was through a dream—not the real world—ultimately revealing the name of the Messiah, the Christ child. God uses dreams for great purposes.

> God can do anything He wants; after all, He's God.

How Does God Reveal Visions?

God speaks again and again through dreams and visions, especially in the last days, and Proverbs, the book of wisdom, lets us know how desperately we need vision, which is another word for revelation or God revealing His will. Proverbs 29:18 says,

> "Where there is no revelation (vision), the people cast off restraint." (NIV)

Vision is a "preferred future." God is saying that we need His vision! We need His view of a preferred future. If we don't have His vision we will crash and burn, so to say. This Proverb is saying that if you do not have God's vision for your life, then you will do whatever you want, casting off restraint. That means living a random life, in chaos and unbelief, living without focus and certainly with the absence of God guiding you and revealing His will for you.

Make no mistake about it—God has a vision for your life. He has a vision for your marriage. God has a vision for your family, and a vision for your career. And He wants to reveal that vision to you.

In 1999, my church found a beautiful piece of property on the Central Coast of California. It was 63 acres of rolling hills and a plateau that overlooked the city. We began the journey of casting vision, meeting with government authorities, raising money, doing extensive environmental studies and impact reports, and it took us ten years to accomplish the mission of having a church facility that we could call home.

Today, thousands of lives are touched through ministry that is facilitated through that property. Marriages are renewed, teenager's lives are transformed, struggling families are getting food assistance, children are being taught the goodness of God—lives are being changed. However, the ten years of getting to the top of our mountain were grueling years, striving through the pain of perseverance. Though for me personally, it was a vision that God had given me in my mind's eye in the year 2000. It was simply a picture of me as an old man, standing in the church building, tears in my eyes, and the whisper of God, "It was worth it." That vision kept me going. I didn't know if it meant that we wouldn't get to the new land until I was an old man! Yet, all I knew was that whenever we got there I would look back and know that it was all worth it. It was God's way of revealing His will with the message "do not grow weary in doing good." I needed that vision. That vision in my mind's eye kept me moving forward when I felt like quitting. That vision gave me hope of a preferred future. That vision lifted me up and over the obstacles that were in our way. And I look forward with great anticipation to someday be an old man (*I don't consider myself an old man quite yet!*) and know that it was all worth it. God speaks through visions.

Make no mistake about it—God has a vision for your life.

So far we have explored four of the five major ways that God speaks to us—which all a part of the God Factor. God speaks primarily through <u>His Word,</u> and all other ways are always in light of God's word, never contradicting His Word. God will use certain <u>people</u> in one's life to reveal His will. God does something on the inside of us, revealing His will through deep <u>conviction and impressions</u>. God tells us that <u>dreams and visions</u> are alive and active.

We now journey to the fifth destination of how God primarily speaks to us to reveal His will for our lives. We have all heard of the expression, "No pain – no gain." This next chapter may be the most difficult, as we discover that God speaks to us through pain. As you read this book, you may be going through an excruciating painful time. But you must read on. God is speaking to you, and *He always has a redeeming purpose in every pain.* The fifth major way that God speaks to us is through pain.

Factor Two: The GOD Factor
Five Ways God Speaks to Us
Fifth Way

Chapter 10
Through Pain

"It was good for me to be afflicted so that I may learn your decrees."
Psalm 119:71 (NIV)

We had three small children, two toddlers and a baby, and my wife was having horrific stomach pain—the kind of pain that has you toppled over for hours upon end. We landed in the hospital for what was called "a routine check up," in an effort to diagnose the problem.

As I sat in the waiting room of the hospital, the doctor told me that she would be out in about a half hour. Three hours later, I am pacing back in forth, wondering, "Why in the world is this taking so long? What was going on? Was there a problem?"

The doctors finally emerged from behind the doors and told me that my wife had an allergic reaction to the iodine that they were pumping through her veins during a CAT scan procedure. Her throat started to swell and she wasn't able to breathe. Like a scene in your favorite emergency room TV show, she immediately was surrounded with doctors and nurses, giving her oxygen and a shot, preserving her life. I was undone. My wife had already had an emergency appendectomy and with three small kids, we were in the thick of it. I wasn't sure how much more I could take. The doctors secured my wife in a room, and I trudged through the parking lot of the hospital and climbed into my car. I was defeated and left to return by myself to my three daughters, who were staying with a friend. I put my head down on the steering wheel and began to cry. Gathering myself, I cried out to God, "Where are You?!" As I shouted that prayer, I turned on the ignition of my car, and in that exact moment the radio was blasting the words in a song, "God is in control!" I was stunned. I cried out in my pain — and God answered me with a loving reminder that He, in fact, was in control. That come what may, He is never caught off guard or surprised. He was saying to me that there was a purpose in my pain, and in my wife's pain. He hadn't left us alone. God had a purpose.

God Speaks Through Pain

God speaks through pain. The trials of life are more than just hurdles that set you back. Pain is the fifth primary way used by God to speak to us. To know God's will, it is vital to understand how God speaks through the pain of our lives. The Almighty wants us to recognize that He has a purpose in everything. As I have told my church countless times, "There is a purpose in every pain."

God loves you so much—He doesn't want to waste anything. He doesn't want the pain of your life leaving you as a beat up casualty. The Prophet Isaiah tells us in Isaiah 61:3 that God *"gives beauty for ashes."* (NIV) He wants to take something *redeeming* out of your painful experiences for your good.

Romans 8:28 reminds us what we should "know." That passage says,

> "And we know that in all things God works
> for the good of those who love him, who have
> been called according to his purpose." (NIV)

There are a lot of "gold nuggets" in that verse, yet perhaps the shiniest gem is the phrase *in all things*. That would mean God uses everything in your life—all things—to shape you for the good.

Being shaped for our good is something God does out of His mercy. Where grace means, "getting something I don't deserve," mercy means, "NOT getting what I do deserve." When God's people begin to journey off the path and begin to play outside the lines, He has a gracious way to lead us back to the path that leads to life. He will allow us to experience pain so that we will turn back to what is good, right, and true.

I remember reading a quote from a NFL professional football player that seemed to have it all—fame, fortune, and so on. He had wandered from truth and was living out of control. He ended up having a critical injury that had him lying on the bed in hospital room, staring at the ceiling. He said, "I was so prideful. God had to finally get me flat on my back so I would look up to Him."

A great example of how God uses pain can even be stubbing your toe! I was in a hurry and racing out of the house, barefoot of all things, and caught my toe on a door. A shockwave of pain riveted through my body! I began to freeze up, paralyzed in pain, and went into Christian cussing—the kind where you squeal, grunt, and huff. (Of course, I have a friend who says to me in those moments, "Jesus knows what you said in your heart.") I know exactly what my friend was talking about. You have probably been there, too.

It is interesting how pain can make us change our ways. Because my toe became black and blue and was throbbing, I am now choosing to not be in a hurry and run around barefoot!

> When God's people begin to journey off the path and begin to play outside the lines, He has a gracious way to lead us back to the path that leads to life.
> He will allow us to experience pain so that we will turn back to what is good, right, and true.

Proverbs 20:30 speaks of this reality:

"Wounds cleanse away evil." (NIV)

This is the idea that when we experience pain, it makes us change our minds, our ways, and who we are at the core of our spiritual being.

To be clear, God is not out to hurt you. However, He uses pain in our lives. I have heard countless stories of people who experienced pain that acted as a "wake-up" call to turn their life over to God.

The Psalmist confesses his "wake-up call" in Psalm 119:67, 71,

> "Before I was afflicted I went astray but now I obey your word... It was good for me to be afflicted so that I may learn your truth." (NIV)

He is basically saying that he found himself wandering off the path, making horrible choices, and when suffering came into his life, he paid attention to God's truth.

If you begin getting off God's path, He will allow you to experience pain, with the purpose of getting you back on the right track. It is out of His love and mercy that He allows you to experience pain, because He's trying to protect you from a devastating crash. It's like the side rails that are strategically positioned on Highway 1 as you drive up the California coast. Those guardrails are not there to spoil your fun, your view, or your Sunday drive. They are there to protect you from rolling your car off the cliff! God speaks through pain to get us on the right road.

In the Midst of a Painful Season

What should you do if you are in the midst of a painful season? The pain can come in various forms whether it is physical trials, emotional stress, or spiritual battles. God wants us to never retreat from Him.

1 Peter 4:19 says,

> "So then, those who suffer according to God's will should commit themselves to their faithful Creator and continue to do good." (NIV)

"God's will" could involve suffering because of the greater good. Think about the suffering of Jesus and the greater good that resulted.

Hebrews 12:3 reminds us,

> "Consider him who endured such opposition from sinners, so that you will not grow weary and lose heart." (NIV)

Jesus endured tremendous suffering! His pain was perhaps the most horrific imaginable. Perhaps you have wondered, "If God the Father loved Him, how could He allow it?" The answer is because there was a greater purpose—the greatest purpose. His suffering means that the price of your sin has been paid for and you get an eternity with Him in heaven.

See the Bigger Picture

Maybe your life has been like Joseph's life in the Old Testament as found in Genesis 37. Joseph was abused. He was betrayed by family members, mistreated by authority, and lied about. He spent time in prison and served as a slave. Joseph simply remained faithful to God and trusted that He was ultimately in control. Later in his life, when his brothers who betrayed him came back into his world asking for help and supplies—though they did not know they were speaking to the brother they beat and sold into slavery— Joseph gave them an amazing response. It is the kind of response that can change your life—if you grab a hold of it. Joseph said to his brothers, "What you meant for harm, God intended for my good."

Joseph had endured horrific pain, yet had the incredible ability to see the greater purpose and all that God was speaking. Could you imagine what he was feeling while sitting in a cold, isolated jail cell? Yet, Joseph could see the bigger picture and knew God was in it. When you and I can understand that God even uses the difficult times of our life for a greater purpose, we will then begin to step into His will for our lives.

You need to know God does speak. He speaks through a number of ways. God speaks primarily through His Word, and all other ways must line up with His Word. Yet God will use people, conviction and impressions, dreams and visions, and the pain of life. Ultimately, God wants you to know His Will for your life. I challenge you today to begin to listen and begin to understand. God is speaking.

> When you and I can understand that God even uses the difficult times of our life for a greater purpose, we will then begin to step into His will for our lives.

**Factor Two: The GOD Factor—
Five Ways God Speaks To Us
First Way: His Word
Second Way: Through Other People
Third Way: Via Conviction and Impressions
Fourth Way: In Dreams and Visions
Fifth Way: Through Pain**

Factor One is **The YOU Factor**. It is all about getting ready to hear from God. Factor Two is **The GOD Factor**. This factor is critical to understand the five primary ways that God speaks to us.

We now delve into Factor Three: **The GOD and YOU Factor** which means literally receiving an answer from God.

Every relationship requires communication. As the saying goes, "It takes two to tango." It also takes two to talk. God is God, and you are you, and God wants to give you answers. So how do you get your answer? Chapters 11 through 15 give a step-by-step practical guide on actually receiving God's direction. Each chapter builds on the other. Let's grab a hold of Factor Three!

Factor Three:
The GOD and YOU Factor
Receiving an Answer from God

"I will look to see what <u>He</u> will say to <u>me</u>…"
Habakkuk 2:1 (NIV)

Step One: Find a Quiet Space

Chapter 11
Finding a Quiet Space

"²He leads me beside quiet waters,
³He refreshes my soul." Psalm 23:2-3a (NIV)

There was a man who lost a valuable watch while working in an icehouse where the floor was filled with sawdust. He and his coworkers raked through the sawdust, but couldn't find it. A little boy heard what was happening, slipped into the icehouse and came out with the watch. All the men were amazed. "How'd you do that?!" they asked. The boy explained, "I closed the door, lay down in the sawdust, and kept very still. Soon I heard the watch ticking." Often the question is not whether God is speaking, but whether we are still enough to hear.

Songwriter Michael John Poitier wrote a beautiful song called, "Come to the Quiet." That is great language, as God gives each of us an invitation to enter into His quieting presence, where in that holy stillness there is a sense of His awesome nearness. That's what it means to find a quiet place with God.

We Live in a Crowded and Noisy World

We live in a very loud world with a multitude of distractions vying for our attention. What does it mean to find a quiet space? It may mean a walk on the beach, a drive up a highway, a room where you can turn off your cell phone, your computer, your tablet, your laptop, your TV, your... your... your... you name it, and quiet *your* soul.

Jesus modeled a way of entering a quiet space. He would retreat into the mountains to hide from the noise of the daily routine. In that place he would pray and listen for his Father's voice.

> Often the question is not whether God is speaking, but whether we are still enough to hear.

Most Americans struggle with finding a quiet place with God because we are bombarded with so much noise and so many distractions. Most people are on the treadmill of life and it doesn't seem like anyone is getting off soon. In fact, in our culture it is celebrated to be busy! I cannot count how many times I have overheard conversations, and sadly even participated in conversations, where the only thing stated was how consumed our lives are. "How's it going?" says one casual friend. The response is, "Busy. You?" The person replies, "Yep, me too—real busy." It seems almost comical, yet sadly this is a major hindrance to encountering God's voice in your life. As one fiery preacher blasted, "If the devil can't make you sin, he'll make you busy!" Perhaps there is truth in that, if busyness really is carrying us further away from the quiet place where God speaks.

Being Too Busy Could Rob You from Understanding God's Will for Your Life

Being too busy could rob you from understanding God's will for your life. We all have worthy things to spend our time on; however, if we can't pull away and find the quiet— we will miss the whispers of God.

Finding a quiet place can mean reflecting on His creation. My wife and I sat on the beach one night and watched the sun set. It was absolutely gorgeous. It made me wonder why we don't watch sunsets more often!

This particular night the sun was a fiery orange ball, making the whole sky glow, as it slipped into the horizon. It was one of those sunsets that made you feel the awesomeness of God. It would be difficult for a person to watch how that sunset painted the sky and to dismiss it as random chance.

> We all have worthy things to spend our time on; however,
> if we can't pull away and find the quiet—
> we will miss the whispers of God.

The Psalmist proclaimed in Psalm 50:1-2,

> "¹The Mighty One, God, the LORD, speaks and summons the earth from the rising of the sun to the place where it sets. ² From Zion, perfect in beauty, God shines forth." (NIV)

God is calling to every human being throughout the earth. His perfection and beauty are on display. He shines forth giving light and splendor for all to see. You may need to go and watch a sunset and let God's awesomeness overtake you!

There Is Strength in a Quiet and Worshipful Place

I have found that when I find a quiet worshipful place with God I feel His strength. I was on a long bike ride all by myself and had what I like to call, a "God-moment." The sun was beaming down, I could smell the nearby lake, and feel the light of the sun glistening off the water. With all of this going on, I was blaring worship music. The only thing that could potentially ruin my "worship nature moment" was my attempt to bicycle uphill on a significant incline (that or a flat tire, of course). Let's just say that some uphill rides are not so joyful! But I burst into a worship song at the top of my lungs, and in that moment it was just the Lord and me. With a huge smile on my face, I raced up the incline with renewed energy and strength.

The experience made me think of the power of worshipping God when we are all alone. When life is noisy and we find ourselves going through uphill trials, we need to find the quiet place and worship the Lord, letting that joy give us strength to endure. Worship is not for us, it's all for Him; yet it is also true that the Lord blesses us in worship.

Psalm 100:2, 5 says,

> "Worship the LORD with gladness; come before him with joyful songs... For the LORD is good and his love endures forever; His faithfulness continues through all gener-ations." (NIV)

When you recognize that you are in the fast lane of life, and you can see that your incline is steep, in that moment come to the quiet and worship God joyfully because His love and faithfulness is extended to you. What you will find is that the quiet place will grant you strength for the journey.

The good news is that God is always available in the quiet places. We can come to Him every day; He's always listening, and in those times we can pour out our hearts.

We need to find the quiet place with God where we can be still and know He is God. Finding the quiet is discovering a safe place that will position us to hear God's whispers, nudges, convictions, and impressions.

Can you be still and hear the watch ticking in the sawdust like the little boy? Can you find the quiet? Well, once you find the quiet, take the next step which is to stay there.

The good news is that God is always available in the
quiet places. We can come to Him every day;
He's always listening, and in those times
we can pour out our hearts.

Factor Three:
The GOD and YOU Factor
Receiving an Answer from God
Step Two: Await the Call Patiently

Chapter 12
Awaiting the Call Patiently

"I will wait to see what He will say to me."
Habakkuk 2:1 (NIV)

William Wallace, the famed warrior who fought for Scotland's independence in the 13th Century, rallied ragtag farmers to do battle against the well trained and heavily armed English army. History says that these peasant military troops hid in the grass, listening to the voice of their leader. Wallace cried out, "Wait for it... wait for it... wait for it... NOW!" The army rose up at the perfect time to attack and defeat the polished soldiers in that battle. They waited and then acted.

Timing Is Everything

It has been said that, "timing is everything." Waiting for God's answer is an issue of timing. As you come to that quiet place with God, you may have to stay there awhile, and that takes waiting and patience.

There is a discipline of waiting and patience. I grew up with my dad always saying, "Patience is a virtue," to the point where my brothers and sister and me would *mouth it* as he would say it. Though whether I want to admit it or not, my dad was right! Patience is a virtue. Patience is a good thing and waiting on God for an answer takes patience. We need to hang in, hold on, and wait patiently for God to give us an answer.

Waiting for God's answer is an issue of timing.

The prophet, Habakkuk, proclaimed,

> "I will wait to see what he will say to me."
> (Habakkuk 2:1 NIV; underline added for emphasis)

Habakkuk was determined to wait on God, and to wait on God for a purpose. The ultimate purpose was to find out how God was going to direct him.

Another prophet, Isaiah, writes,

> "But those who wait on the LORD, shall renew their strength; they shall mount up with wings like eagles, they shall run and not be weary, they shall walk and not faint."
> (Isaiah 40:31 NKJV; underline added for emphasis)

We need to understand that waiting on God, waiting before the Lord of the universe, waiting on the great Creator of all things, produces good things in our lives. When we wait on God, it gives us freedom to fly, strength to run, and the endurance to not quit. Our part is to be still and wait on God.

Be Patient before God

We live in a microwave world where we want things as quickly as possible. Yet, God calls us to be patient before Him. Our culture seems to have changed the motto of "stop and smell the roses" to "why stop and smell the roses when you can drive right through them!" Waiting on God flows against what most of us are used to. To get God's answer you will have to swim against the current and wait quietly for Him to guide.

When waiting the call of God patiently, always remember three things: God always sees you, always hears you, and always has a redemptive plan.

> Waiting on God flows against
> what most of us are used to.

There will be times when it feels as if your prayers are bouncing off the ceiling. Those are the times when it is easy to question if God is even there. As you wait patiently, never ever forget that God always sees you, hears you, and has a redemptive plan.

When communication in a relationship comes to a halt, it leaves a person wondering. Many times we can take communicating with God for granted. We slowly slip into the sin of familiarity.

This truth came home to me when my daughter was working with an organization called Youth With A Mission (YWAM) and was ministering overseas. We had been emailing daily, calling each other on the Internet once a week, and staying in close communication.

Then she and her YWAM team went on a two week outreach trip to a remote island that doesn't have Internet service! All communication came to a screeching halt!

It can be so easy for any of us to take communication for granted—especially in the high-tech world we live in. We can even take "communication" with the Lord for granted.

The good news is that God does not require email service, cell phone coverage, or satellite. We can come to Him every day; He's always listening, and in those times we can communicate with Him, though, it's easy to get running so fast that we don't.

That was like my friend who was heading for a destination and to get there he needed to drive through Yosemite National Park in California, one of the most breathtaking places in the world. He was pressing the speed limit and taking on a frenetic pace. All of a sudden he had that "God nudge" of "What in the world are you doing?" His attempt to blast through at mach speed was making him miss the grandeur of God's creation. He immediately and purposely pulled the car over to the side of the road and drank in the Lord's beauty in creation. He created space to wait patiently before the Almighty and pour his heart out to Him. We need to do this, too.

The Third Factor is all about receiving an answer from God—it's **The GOD and YOU Factor**. Receiving your answer from God requires finding a quiet place and awaiting the call patiently, which leads to the next step—the art of listening for His voice. Get ready to tune in!

Factor Three:
The GOD and YOU Factor
Receiving an Answer from God
Step Three: Listen for His Voice

Chapter 13
Listening for His Voice

"My sheep listen to my voice." John 10:27 (NIV)

Married with two small children, I was struggling to get a new business off the ground, working out of my garage and not fully confident I would be able to support my family through this start-up. The phone rang. It was the local school district calling to offer me a job. So much was racing through my mind in a quick two-minute conversation. I was being offered a job that would provide insurance for my family, a steady income, and a job that I would really enjoy. I paused for as long as I could, quietly asking God what I should do. It was like a whisper to my heart, "Don't take the job." I probably stuttered while responding to the school official, "Tha-tha-tha-thank you, but I will need to decline."

Listen for God's Voice—He Will Answer

I was listening for God's voice, and He answered. It seemed like a strange answer and didn't totally make sense. Taking the job could have been the logical choice, the prudent choice for that stage of my life. I even walked back into the house from the garage to tell my wife. I said, *"I just got offered a job by the school district."* She said, *"That's awesome!"* I said, *"And I declined it."* And she replied, *"That's interesting."* When I told my wife how I paused in silence and really looked to listen for God's voice, I felt His response. She concluded it was the right decision then.

The fascinating part of the rest of the story is that within nine months of the offer, jobs were slashed at the school district over budget cuts and the position I was offered was cancelled. However my business went on to provide for my family, though at the time I had no clue, no indication that it would. I trusted His voice over just going with the flow. We all can have ups and downs with job opportunities, yet this was a lesson of intentionally listening for God's will.

The Art of Learning to Hear God's Voice

Learning to hear God's voice is an art, yet it can be learned. Jesus said His sheep would know the shepherd's voice. God's voice is active; He can speak very loudly and even can speak in silence. In the previous two chapters we recognized that it is so important to find a quiet space and await God's answers patiently, which positions us to hear His voice. The prophet Habakkuk knew that he had to learn the art of how God would answer, as he says in Habakkuk 2:1c in the Old Testament,

> "I will wait to <u>learn how God will answer</u> my complaint."
> (NIV; underline added for emphasis)

God's voice is active.

Habakkuk says, "I'll learn," which means he will be teachable, try to recognize how God will answer, and wait for it. Habakkuk had put in a "complaint" to God, or what might also be called a "request" to God. The question became, "How will God answer that request?" A critical part of the answer to that question is to listen for His voice. If you do not have much experience with "listening for His voice" just be like Habakkuk—be a learner! Practice listening for God's voice. He will surprise you.

This came home to me years ago when I walked into a large store and started to make my way up to the customer service counter. I was looking at how huge the store building was and found myself wondering what God was up to in this massive space with people everywhere. So I said a little prayer, still approaching the customer service counter, "God, what are you doing in this building?" A still small voice spoke in the quiet place of my heart, "Her name is Gayle." The woman at the customer service counter, whose back was to me, turned around to help me, and her nametag said, "Gayle." I was in shock! I am not suggesting that God will tell you names of people—in fact this was the only time this ever happened in my life. The point is: God was teaching me another lesson. If I would inquire what is His will and what He is doing, then He would answer.

The Psalmist had incredible confidence that God would answer him, because he had incredible confidence that God loved him, desiring to reveal His will for his life.

Psalm 17:6-7 says,

> "I call on you, O God, <u>for you will answer
> me</u>; give ear to me and hear my prayer.
> Show the wonder of your great love."
> (NIV; underline added for emphasis)

God wants us to have that confidence. *You need to believe* that God desires to give you the answers that you are searching for. Listening for His voice is the best way to demonstrate that you believe God wants to answer you.

You may not get a quick answer. That's why we need to "learn" how God will speak to us. Jesus did teach the idea of "pressing in" and persevering for an answer. He said in Matthew 7:7-8,

> "[7]Ask and it will be given to you; seek and
> you will find; knock and the door will be
> opened to you. [8] For <u>everyone who asks
> receives</u>; he who seeks <u>finds</u>; and to him who
> knocks, the door will be <u>opened</u>."
> (NIV; underlines added for emphasis)

You need to believe that God desires to give you the answers that you are searching for.

God Invites You to Ask Questions

God invites you to ask questions. He is not bothered by it. When you are asking God questions, this is a form of seeking and knocking. Have you ever been around an inquisitive toddler, where they constantly are asking "why" questions? After awhile you run out of answers that will surrender to their onslaught of questions. At this point, you throw your hands up and cry out, "I don't know why?!"

To be clear, God never gets frustrated with our questions… and invites you to ask away! But we do need to learn how he speaks. Remember Factor Two, The GOD Factor and how God speaks to us. He speaks to us primarily through His Word, and through people, conviction, impressions, vision, dreams, and even pain. Sometimes it may seem like God is being silent, but he even communicates through silence. As a mentor of mine told me a long time ago, when we ask God a question, He typically has three answers: "yes, no, or wait." When God is being silent, this could be His answer to "wait." God is not ignoring us, though He is allowing us to trust and wait, which, whether we like it or not, always builds character.

I read an article about a guy who is called the Chess Master. He is a sought after mentor and teacher of the game of chess. The Chess Master instructed on the power of silence, "My lessons consist of a lot of silence. I let my students think. If I do ask a question and I don't get the right answer, I'll rephrase the question and wait. I never give the answer. Most of us really don't appreciate the power of silence. Some of the most effective communication between student and teacher, between master players takes place during silent periods."

Learn How God Will Speak and then Listen

God is our ultimate mentor and teacher, and He too, can communicate volumes through silence. Our part is to do what the Old Testament prophet Habakkuk did... learn how God will speak and then listen. That will lead you to the next step, a step that Habakkuk did as well. He wrote down God's message. It's time to pull out your yellow pad and pen, your laptop, or your tablet, whatever works for you, and discover the power of writing down God's message.

> God is our ultimate mentor and teacher...
> learn how God will speak and then listen.

Factor Three:
The GOD and YOU Factor
Receiving an Answer from God
Step Four: Write the Message Down

Chapter 14
Writing the Message Down

"The LORD answered me: 'Write down the vision;
write it clearly...'"
Habakkuk 2:2 (NIV)

As I have mentioned, ever since 1992 I make the week between Christmas Day and New Year's Day my vision week. I get up early, grab my coffee, and sit down with a pen and yellow note pad, looking to see what God would show me for the coming year. I reflect on the past year, and get vision for what is coming. It's one of my favorite times of the year... just me and my yellow pad (and my cup of coffee)!

The Lord giving direction to a person is so incredibly spiritual. Writing the answer down on paper is so incredibly practical. There is something wonderful and powerful about writing down God's message to us. When we write down important things, it leads to having clarity and the ability to reference it over and over again. When a person writes down God's answer, they can refer to it and this helps overcome doubt.

Overcoming Whispers of Doubt

There will always be whispers of doubt that zip through your mind. Those doubts have the message that says, "Did God say?" It is the same trick that the serpent used with Adam and Eve that is described in Genesis 3:1. The snake squirmed its way in and said, "Did God say, 'Do not eat of the fruit?'" We can have the same doubts enter our minds. There will be times where things may not be coming together and we question God's direction. However, when we have something written down that we can refer to, it becomes a powerful reminder that encourages us to press on.

> The Lord giving direction to a person is so incredibly spiritual. Writing the answer down on paper is so incredibly practical.

Writing Down What God Inspires You To Do Is Spiritual and Practical

The Old Testament prophet Habakkuk took hold of this spiritual and practical discipline as he cries out,

> "The LORD answered me: 'Write down the vision; write it clearly...'" Habakkuk 2:2
> (NIV; underline added for emphasis)

When the LORD answers us, having that still small voice operating in our lives is so incredibly spiritual. To Habakkuk, it was as if God was saying, "Write the answer, the vision, write it clearly so you have clarity and so you can reference it over and over."

God calls us to have "reminders!" In Proverbs 7:2-3, He tells us,

> "¹Follow my advice...always treasure my commands. ² Obey them and live! Guard my teachings as your most precious possession. ³ Tie them on your fingers as a <u>reminder</u>. Write them deep within your heart."
> (NLT; underline added for emphasis)

When God gives you advice, follow it. When He gives a command, obey it. When the Lord brings a teaching, treasure it. When the book of wisdom says, "Tie them on your fingers as a reminder," that means *do something* that will remind you of God's instruction!

The Most Important Writing Is Written in the Heart

I would highly encourage you to write it all down, and if you do, that will lead to possibly the most important writing you have ever done. It will lead toward having the message written deep in your heart. Let God's Word get into the deepest place of who you are. As one of my mentors told me years ago, "If you hear something, you will likely forget it. If you write it down, you will likely remember it. If you do it, you will learn it."

God calls us to have "reminders!"

Hear, Write, and Do

Notice the progression of that insight: hear, write, and do. Writing God's direction is the "bridge" to actualizing it, to walking it out.

This may sound crazy to you, yet every huge decision I have made in my life has come through a yellow note pad. I say with all reverence, it's the other "holy" trinity—You, God, and your Notepad!

I write the messages I give every Sunday word for word as I sense God's leading and impressions. I used to literally handwrite them, yet because my handwriting is so messy, and one would need the gift of interpretation to read them, I now type them out on my laptop.

Someone asked me years ago about how I put messages together and I told them, "I hand write all my messages and I pray a prayer every week as I go to write, 'Holy Spirit flow through my pen.'" (Then my pen would start to shake... not really, just kidding.) I now pray for the Holy Spirit to flow through my typing on the keypad of my laptop.

The power of writing down God's answers is that you can refer to what you've written, evaluate it, and allow your writing to overcome doubt. This leads to the final step in Factor Three: **The GOD and YOU Factor.** In receiving an answer from God, you must keep your hope alive. God has perfect timing, and that requires hope.

> Let God's Word get into the deepest place of who you are.

Factor Three:
The GOD and YOU Factor
Receiving an Answer from God
Step Five: Keep Your Hope Alive

Chapter 15
Keeping Your Hope Alive

"For the vision awaits an appointed time…"
Habakkuk 2:3 (NIV)

Hope is what keeps you moving forward in life. Famous author and Nazi concentration camp survivor, Victor Frankl, explained the power of hope in his book, *Man's Search for*

Meaning. He emphatically pointed out that the difference between those who endured the horrific conditions of the Nazi prisoner camps, and those who did not, was an issue of hope. The common denominator of those who survived was "hope." They had something to look forward to; something to go home to; something that was waiting for them.

God Is In Control

When it comes to keeping your hope alive, we need to understand God is in control. God has perfect timing. He has an appointed time for certain events in your life. After God gives the answer, our part is to wait for it. That means keeping our hope alive. That means not losing hope. That ultimately means waiting for God to move and fulfill the dream.

Living in the 21st Century we usually don't want to wait for anything. Our culture is not accustomed to waiting, yet God says to wait. We need to be passionate about focusing on hope and waiting for His best, versus trying to force things too soon, and then losing hope.

This is critical to discovering God's will for your life.

Habakkuk 2:3 says,

> "For the vision awaits an appointed time; it speaks of the end and will not prove false. <u>Though it linger, wait for it</u>; it <u>will certainly come</u> and will not delay."
>
> (NIV; underlines added for emphasis)

Wait for His Best

The Lord has an appointed time for the major events of our lives. After God gives the answer, our part is to wait for the events to happen. We are to do our part and walk it out, yet the timing of everything is in God's hands.

Living in our day and age, we don't want to wait for anything! We want to microwave everything. We seem to have this deep-rooted desire for the fast lane so we can speed it up. Our culture's motto seems to be "Move it or lose it!" Our culture is not accustomed to waiting for anything. However, what does God say? He says, "Wait." Wait for His best versus trying to force things where we will ultimately not be satisfied. Wait for his best.

Habakkuk waits for God's best and doesn't lose hope. Why?

He explains in Habakkuk 3:2,

> "I have heard all about you, LORD, and I
> am filled with awe by the <u>amazing things you
> have done</u>."
> (NIV; underline added for emphasis)

He knew the character of the Lord. He stood there blown away in awe. He said, "God you have done amazing things."

The Psalmist cries out in Psalm 25:5,

> "<u>Guide</u> me in your truth and <u>teach</u> me, for
> <u>you are God my Savior</u>, and <u>my hope</u> is in you
> all day long."
> (NIV; underlines added for emphasis)

If you want to know God's will, then you have to know He wants to guide you and teach you. God is your savior, which means He saves you out of situations. The Psalmist knew this and is really saying, *"My hope is in you ALLLLL day long!"*

If you want to know God's will, then you have to know He wants to guide you and teach you.

The Power of Hope

1 Thessalonians 1:3 talks about the power of hope as it says,

> "We continually remember before our God and Father your work produced by <u>faith</u>, your labor prompted by <u>love</u>, and your endurance <u>inspired by hope in our Lord Jesus Christ</u>." (NIV; underlines added for emphasis)

When a person turns his or her life over to God, He gives them an assignment. You need to know that God has a plan for you. He has a good future for you and at the same time, it takes "work and faith"... it takes "labor and love"... and "endurance and hope." You need the "both-and." If it's all work and <u>no</u> faith—you burn out. If it's all labor and <u>no</u> love—you hurt people. If it's all endurance and <u>no</u> hope— it's like being on a treadmill... *forever... an eternal treadmill... no destination... no purpose.* What a bummer for us to labor, work, and endure without a purpose. Life without hope and purpose makes life meaningless.

Your Purpose in Your Generation

God has a purpose for you in your generation, whether you are young or old, or are in between. God has a purpose for you in <u>your generation</u>. I walked into the children's ministry that we call "Kid's Church" and one of the kids shouted out to me in front of everyone, "I saw you on TV!" I had done a spot on television, inviting people to our church. I was kind of caught off guard, so I fired back, "Did I look young or old?" And he said, "In the middle." I thought that was a good answer! That kid is a future politician.

If you are older, God has a purpose for you to invest your life in those younger. You are not through and God is not through with you. If you are young, I'm so excited for you—you need to feel the freedom to dream big and to pursue God's purpose for your life—to go for it! And if you are like me and in the *middle*, well, reach out to everybody you can. God wants to reveal the fullness of His purpose for you.

Scripture reveals to us that God's will for your life requires faith. God's will for your life requires love. God's will for your life needs to be inspired by hope. That means we have to keep our hope alive.

God wants to reveal the fullness of His purpose for you.

Please know that God wants to give you the answer you are searching for. So let me review the five steps that it will take:

1. Find a quiet space.
2. Await the call patiently.
3. Listen for His voice.
4. Write the message down.
5. Keep your hope alive.

If you will take these five steps and walk them out, you will get direction from God and enter into God's will for your life. It all starts with getting some quiet time with God, and ends with keeping your hope alive.

**Factor Three: The GOD and YOU Factor—
Receiving an Answer from God
Step One: Finding a Quiet Space
Step Two: Awaiting the Call Patiently
Step Three: Listening For His Voice
Step Four: Writing the Message Down
Step Five: Keeping Your Hope Alive**

We have journeyed through **The YOU Factor, The GOD Factor,** and **The GOD and YOU Factor.** Now we head into uncharted waters... **The TEST Factor.** The following chapters offer five ways to test what a person may believe is God's will. These next five chapters will bring helpful guidelines for you and empower you to test if the answer is from God, or not! <u>These chapters become your checklist</u>! We now enter into the fourth factor—**The TEST Factor.**

Factor Four:
The TEST Factor
Testing Your Decisions
Test One: Line Your Decisions Up with God's Word

"Test everything..." 1 Thessalonians 5:21 (NIV)

Chapter 16
Lining Up Your Decisions with God's Word

"The word of the Lord stands forever." 1 Peter 1:25
(NIV; underline added for emphasis)

God's will lines up with God's Word. Always. If the answer that you believe is God's will for your life does not agree with God's Word then you can stop right there and know that you have the wrong answer.

There was a woman who said, "God told me that it was okay to hate my husband." I didn't know whether to laugh or cry! One thing I could do was to confidently tell her that "hating her husband" could not be God's will for her life, because God has already told us in His Word that we are to love our spouse, and unconditionally love everyone in the world for that matter.

Examining Emotional Connections and Spiritual Decisions

This woman's problem was that she was emotionally connected to the decision and confused that to be a spiritual one. She was probably in a tumultuous relationship, and emotionally had feelings of hurt and resentment. So for her, it was easy to confuse that God was spiritually giving her the green light to hate her husband. I shudder to think how many things have been done in the name of God that in reality were the furthest thing from God's heart and perfect will. If wars have been created in the name of God, how much more have misguided people tagged God's name on their harmful actions? So it is critical to discern God's will, especially when we are emotionally connected to the decision.

God's Word Divides Heart and Soul

Hebrews 4:12 reveals that God's Word divides heart and soul, or in other words the "spiritual and emotional" elements. This ancient truth says,

> "For the Word of God is living and active. Sharper than any double-edged sword, it penetrates even to dividing soul and spirit, joints and marrow; it judges the thoughts and attitudes of the heart." (NIV)

This is a powerful truth that helps us answer the question, "Is this me and my emotions, or is this God?"

God's will lines up with God's Word. Always.

The word *heart* in the Bible is talking about the *spiritual core* of who you are—the very depth and center of your spiritual being. The word *soul* in the Bible speaks of our *mind, will and emotions.* God's Word has the unique ability to separate or "divide" emotional and spiritual issues, like a scalpel in the hand of a highly skilled surgeon. God's Word carefully and precisely divides issues of the heart and the issues of the soul. Be careful. The more emotionally connected that you are to a decision the more likely it is to confuse God's voice in your life. We desperately need to look at our emotional decisions through the magnified glass of God's Word. It's so true that when dealing with God's will for your life, it is almost always emotional because it is so intertwined with the details, passions, and pursuits of our lives.

Emotions come and go, and are very unpredictable. There aren't many things that will last forever.

However, 1 Peter 1:25 reminds us,

"The <u>Word of the Lord</u> stands forever."
(NIV; underline added for emphasis)

God's Word stands the test of time. Jesus said the earth will pass away, but His words would last forever.

2 Timothy 3:16 explains how God's Word gets us on the path of God's will. It translates,

"All Scripture is inspired by God and is useful to teach us what is true and to make us realize what is wrong in our lives. It straightens us out and teaches us to do what is right." (NLT)

God's will always aligns with His Word. You will find this true as you allow His Word to correct what is wrong in your life. It will teach you to do the right thing that leads you more fully into God's will for your life. Our lives can get tangled, like a ball of yarn, though God's Word wonderfully and graciously pulls that yarn until it is straight, making His will clear.

Do What God's Word Says

Our high calling is to follow the instruction of God's Word. As James 1:22 says,

"Do not merely listen to the Word, and so deceive yourselves. <u>Do what it says</u>."
(NIV; underline added for emphasis)

If you truly want to know God's will for your life, and His Word tells you what to do, then don't ignore it, but do what it says.

Have you ever been ignored by someone? They seem to send the message, "I don't hear you... you don't exist... la la la, I'm tuning you out." That never feels good. Ignoring God's Word is ignoring God, and thus His will for your life.

> God's Word stands the test of time.

During Super Bowl XXXVII, FedEx ran a commercial that spoofed the movie *Castaway* with Tom Hanks. In the ad a FedEx worker plays the role of Tom Hank's long-haired, bearded, island-marooned character. His company plane had gone down, stranding him on a desert island for years. Looking remarkably like the "island-bound" Hanks in the movie, the FedEx employee in the commercial goes up to the door of a suburban home, with a package in hand. When the lady comes to the door, he explains that he survived five years on a deserted island, and during the whole time he kept this package in order to deliver it to her. She gives a simple, *"Thank you."* Being curious about what is in the package that he has been protecting for years, he says, *"If I may ask, what was in that package after all?"* She opens it and shows him the contents, saying, *"Oh, nothing really. Just a satellite phone, a global positioning device, a compass, a water purifier, and some seeds."* God's Word is your satellite telephone, global positioning device, compass, water purifier, and seeds! His Word is like the contents in this package that has the resources to point us in the right direction. And His truth is available for every person who will take advantage of it.

Just as in this commercial, the package we must open is God's Word, because His will must line up with His Word. Though lining things up with God's Word is a foundational and critical test, there is another step that is more personal: you have to make the right match!

Factor Four:
The TEST Factor
Testing Your Decisions
Test Two: Match Your Gifts

Chapter 17
Matching Your Gifts

"In His grace, God has given us different gifts
for doing certain things well." Romans 12:6 (NLT)

God created you for a certain purpose, and a certain fit. His will is going to match that fit. If you're a sprinter, He doesn't make you run the marathon. If you hate numbers or are horrible at math, God is not willing you to be an accountant. As the saying goes, you can't put a square peg in a round hole. God gives each one of us gifts, abilities, and the grace to do certain things really well. While discovering

God's will for your life, understand this, "His calling matches your gifts!"

His Calling Matches Your Gifts

When I went off to college, I was recruited by the football team and had the blessing to pick any major that I wanted. Someone suggested that I choose engineering, because the university was well known for that major. There was something in me, like a prompting in my soul that just didn't feel right about my gifts and personality being a fit for me to become an engineer. So I trusted that "God nudge" and took another path, finding a major that was a better fit for me. While at the university I confirmed that my decision was the right one as I attempted to take calculus and that turned out to be a disaster! I failed the class and hope I never see another sine or cosine for the rest of my life. (*All the math people out there are laughing at me right now.*) However, my college buddy who attempted to coach me through the calculus class is today a very successful engineer. *Why?* Because God's will for his life matched his gifts and abilities.

If it is true that God's will for your life matches your gifts, then it would be critical to know and understand the gifts He has given you. The following are some guidelines in understanding how "gifts" work and how they fit with your life calling.

> While discovering God's will for your life, understand this, "His calling matches your gifts!"

Your Gifts Are Unique to You

1 Corinthians 12:4-6 tells us,

> "[4]There are <u>different kinds of gifts</u>, but the same Spirit. [5] There are <u>different kinds of service</u>, but the same Lord. [6] There are <u>different kinds of working</u>, but the same God works all of them in all people."
> (NIV; underlines added for emphasis)

There are so many different kinds of gifts, service, and workings that God bestows upon people. He works these many different gifts in all kinds of different people. Your gifts are unique to you, and my gifts are unique to me. Some have teaching gifts, and others administration gifts, and still others have mechanical gifts *and I hate you*. Just kidding—I love you. In fact I need you! Your gifts are *unique*!!

Your Gifts <u>Serve</u> Your Generation

Acts 13:36 talks about David from the Old Testament and gives us a great insight into what our gifts are for. It says,

> "For when David had served God's purpose in his <u>own generation,</u> he fell asleep." (NIV; underline added for emphasis)

I love this verse as it's talking about David who was a passionate shepherd boy and eventually became king. David had very unique gifts: he was a warrior, a musician, a leader, poet, and song writer who penned the majority of the Psalms. Acts 13:36 (NIV) says, "He served God's purpose for *his own generation* and then fell asleep," which means he died. (Italics added for emphasis) *He served his God-given purpose and then kicked it.* That's what I want to do. I want to know God's will for my life, serve my generation with my gifts for the purpose God has given me, and then die and go to heaven.

God has a purpose for you in your generation, and He gives you gifts to fulfill your purpose. Begin to look at the gifts that God has given you and then begin to dream big on how you could impact your generation, the people in your world, your sphere, your family, your neighborhood, and your workplace. Part of God's will for your life, is for you to use your gifts to affect your generation for the good.

Your Gifts Are Shaped by the Events of Your Life

There is a wonderful promise in Romans 8:28 that reminds us,

> "And we know that <u>in all things</u> God works
> for the good of those who love him, who have
> been called according to his purpose."
> (NIV; underline added for emphasis)

God takes the highs and the lows, the hurts and the healings, the failures and the victories and allows your life to be shaped and your gifts to be refined by the events of your life.

I think of what the Bible tells us of the Apostle Paul. God's will for Paul was that he had to speak effectively to Jews and to Gentiles, or non-Jews. The events of his life shaped his teaching gift for each group. In his own words he was a "Hebrew of Hebrews" and at the same time he was a "Roman Citizen." He would have been trained in the Old Testament Law and the Roman educational system as well. What a great candidate to teach both Jews and Gentiles! God uses the events of your life to shape your gifts.

I think of a member at my church who courageously stepped out for a documentary film on growing up in homes with mental illness. Her life was transformed by God's grace after coming to the church, yet her childhood was extremely challenging. Now, like Paul, she is using her gifts, even where there was heartache, and she is walking out God's will for her life and serving His purpose for her generation.

If you look at your life closely, you will begin to see the canvas and colors that God has used to shape you. Gifts are like a paintbrush in God's hands, and He begins to bring color to your life on the canvas of grace. He transforms lives as you use your gifts in your sphere of influence.

Here is one final guideline in understanding how God gives gifts to people to fulfill His will for their life...

God Will *Not* Take Back Your Gifts

Romans 11:29 tells us,

"...for <u>God's gifts</u> and <u>His call</u> are <u>irrevocable</u> (can never be withdrawn)."
(NIV; underlines and parenthetical phrase added for emphasis)

God gives you gifts and they are forever. You may have heard the slogan, *"Diamonds are forever."* Well, God gifts are forever and He doesn't take them back.

You may have blown it in life. You may have done some really "not smart" things, or as the book of Proverbs puts it, "stupid" things! You've got to love Proverbs, using the word *stupid*. Even so, God won't take back His gifts, and He won't take back His call. He invites you to get back on the right path. He invites you to turn from your mistakes. He invites you to leave the mess behind. And in that place He says to you, "You are my workmanship. Let me form you. Let me give you gifts to use for significance!"

> God has a purpose for you in your generation, and He gives you gifts to fulfill your purpose.

Understanding how God's gifts work and relate to His will for your life is huge. His gifts are special and unique to you, and they will serve your purpose for your generation. Also, the gifts God gives are shaped by your life events, and can never be taken away. His gifts are for good.

The fourth factor, **The TEST Factor**, involves lining up God's will for your life with God's Word and then matching your gifts with God's will for your life. This leads us to another step in **The TEST Factor** which will help discern God's will for your life.

With the direction you are sensing from God, ask the question, "Does it help other people?" God always looks to help those in need and we can become His hands and feet to a hurting world. So let's continue to journey through **The TEST Factor**, testing our decisions.

Factor Four:
The TEST Factor
Testing Your Decisions
Test Three: Help Others

Chapter 18
Helping Others

"Love your neighbor as yourself."
Mark 12:31 (NIV)

When walking out Factor Four: **The TEST Factor**, God's will lines up with His Word, it matches your gifts, and then it should center on helping others. Why is that? God blesses a person to be a blessing. God calls us to help everyone that we can. Part of discerning God's will for our lives is understanding that God's will for our lives will actually help other people.

What Is Success?

When looking at God's will for your life, most people want to be successful in what they are pursuing. Yet that forces a great question. *What is success?* Anyone can define success in any way they want. For some, it is fame and fortune, and for others it may be just trying to be happy. For some, success may be power and for others it could mean doing the least amount of work possible— *"Hakuna Matada... it's a trouble free philosophy!"* For others, it means climbing the corporate ladder and being the best. So, a person can aim for success and believe that success, however they define it, is God's will for their life.

When I was in the 5th Grade I wrote a report on what I would be when I grew up, or in other words, "What I thought was God's will for my life." I still have that report with color drawings to boot. I was going to be the quarterback for an NFL football team. I was going to be married with eight kids—four boys and four girls. I was going to drive a Corvette—which back then cost $10,000 and everyone asked, "Who would ever pay $10,000 for a car?!" How I would fit those eight kids in that Corvette? I don't know! Well, I'm not the quarterback for an NFL team, I don't have four boys and four girls, and I don't drive a Corvette. *Did I miss God's will for my life!* How do you define success? God defines it by helping others.

> God blesses a person to be a blessing.

God Defines Success as Helping Others

God has a different way of looking at things. His Word talks about having a whole different worldview, a different way of looking at life and how we spend our time, energy, and money. God could care less how the world defines success. God's will for our lives revolves around significance. Significance is helping other people. God's will for your life, is about helping other people.

Jesus asked a question in Mark 8:36,

"What good is it for a man to gain the whole world, yet forfeit his soul?" (NIV)

In this statement, Jesus lays everything out on the table. He suggests if someone were to gain the whole world, that is to say have all the money, all the power, all the pleasure you can think of, and sells his soul to get it, in the end what does he have? Nothing. Because this life on earth is a second, a snap, a flash, *compared to eternity.* Do you want to forfeit your soul and gain the whole world for two seconds and then miss out on God's will for your life? So the question simply becomes, *"What am I living for? What am I doing with my life?"*

We can learn from David in the Old Testament as he writes in Psalm 39 a powerful description of viewing life, God's will, and making a difference. It seems that David is so passionate about the subject that he is like a volcano, waiting to blow. As you read his words, there is this rumbling going on as he is looking at life here on earth and he's trying to hold back his feelings, and then the volcano blows! David lets it all out. He was an observer of life and he was also "off-the-charts" passionate. He was giving thought to what was happening in his day, in his world, and what he could do about it. It was a thought process that began with a frustration with the world around him.

David erupts in Psalm 39:1-3,

> "[1]I said, 'I will watch my ways and keep my tongue from sin; I will put a muzzle on my mouth as long as the wicked are in my presence.' [2] But when I was silent and still, not even saying anything good, my anguish increased. [3] My heart grew hot within me, and as I meditated, the fire burned; then I spoke with my tongue." (NIV)

David says, "As I meditated—the fire burned." He's trying to keep a check on his own life; he's trying to be careful of what he says and keeping his mouth in check. So he stays silent, yet the fire burns within him. Then the volcano blew! He was frustrated with the evil things that were going on around him. There was frustration with evil people, frustration over the weak being oppressed, and he couldn't stand it anymore.

Usually when someone does something—about something that is going on that is *not* right—there is an inner verbal progression! They say to themselves,

> "You know what is happening over there is wrong—**someone** should do something about it... you know, what is happening over there is wrong—**you** should do something about it... you know, what is happening over there is wrong—**I** should do something about it... you know, what is happening over there is wrong—**I have to** do something about it!"

And they go do something about it. Whether it's educating children, stopping drugs in their community, feeding the hungry, leading those who are spiritually dead to relationship with God—people of significance see the need and do something about it.

Part of God's will for your life is that you would get passionate like David, see the need, and erupt into action; because God's will for your life will center around helping others.

In Psalm 39, not only is David seeing and feeling the atrocities that are happening in the world where he begins to burn inside with frustration, he then adds the reality of reflecting on the brevity of life.

He continues to pen in Psalm 39:4-5,

"⁴Show me, O LORD, my life's end and the number of my days; let me know how fleeting is my life. ⁵ You have made my days a mere handbreadth; the span of my years is as nothing before you. Each man's life is but a breath." (NIV)

His thoughts turned on the shortness of life and on the mystery of the divine arrangement by which it is made so short. You have seen the slogan, *"Life is short—play hard."* I might change that to, *"Life is short—PRAY hard!"*

Life is but a breath. Another scripture says that life is a vapor, here today and then gone. When I think of vapor I think of the steam that raised off my coffee cup this morning—poof! And it was gone. God is saying that all of time is swallowed up in His eternity. This truth is a warning, "Never waste a heartbeat... Life is too short... Never waste a heartbeat."

> ...people of significance see the need and do the something about it.

Helping Others Is the Opposite of How Most of the World Defines Success

Helping others is the opposite of how most of the world defines success. For many, success and accomplishments are defined by money and busyness.

David observes the nature of many people in Psalm 39:6,

> "Man is a mere phantom as he goes to and fro: He bustles about, but only in vain; he heaps up wealth, not knowing who will get it." (NIV)

People moving around like a phantom or shadow is another way of saying, "Not living in reality." Bustling about and creating commotion, doing a lot of activity for activity's sake, and making a buck here and there while not knowing who will get it, by definition, is purposeless.

From the 1849 California Gold Rush to the Dot.Com rush, it was all about "gold fever, baby." Listen, it's great to work hard, be productive, and be prosperous. If you are in business, the goal of business is to make money and be profitable. If that is not your goal, you probably shouldn't be in business. Yet, how great would it be to make money to help others! Whether God calls you to be the butcher, the baker, or the candlestick maker, His will for your life will focus on helping other people.

When David said, "...he goes to and fro... bustles about," that sounds like 21st Century America to me! Helping others isn't about making ourselves overly busy. I am just as guilty as the next person. People ask me, "How's it going?" And at times I will reply, "BUSY... real busy." As if to pat myself on the back in some warped way that busyness *validates* me. Let me clarify, whatever you do—work hard at it. Give your very best. But in no way get your value, your affirmation, or your worth from strokes of being *busy*.

"How Can I Make a Difference?"

God wants to bless you and prosper you, but not for the sake of "what can I get out of it," rather, "how can I make a difference?!" Toys and nice cars are gifts from God; they're blessings though He calls us to keep it all in perspective and answer the bigger question, "How can I make a difference?" When we focus on making a difference and helping others there is a sense of significance and meaning to life. Victor Frankl offers incredible insight on the meaning of life, as he drew from unbelievable life circumstances.

When the Nazis in World War II arrested Victor Frankl, he was stripped of everything, including his family, property, and possessions. Researching and writing for years on the topic of the importance of finding meaning in life, he arrived at the death camp, Auschwitz, and his manuscript, which he had hidden in the lining of his coat, was confiscated. He penned, "I found myself confronted with the question of whether under such circumstances my life was ultimately void of any meaning." Grappling with that question, a few days later when the Nazis forced the prisoners to give up their clothes, he wrote,

> "I had to surrender my clothes and in turn inherited the worn out rags of an inmate who had been sent to the gas chamber. Instead of

the many pages of my manuscript, I found in the pocket of the newly acquired coat a single page torn out of a Hebrew prayer book, which read, 'Hear, O Israel! The Lord our God is one God. And you shall love the Lord your God with all your heart and with all your soul and with all your might.' How should I have interpreted such a 'coincidence' other than as a challenge to 'live' my thoughts instead of merely putting them on paper?"

Later, as Frankl reflected on his ordeal, he wrote in his book *Man's Search for Meaning*, "There is nothing in the world that would so effectively help one to survive even the worst conditions, as the knowledge that there is a meaning in one's life... He who has a 'why' to live for can bear almost any 'how'."

When searching for the meaning of life, and even God's will for your life, remember the *why* will center on helping others. People of significance care about other people, and always are looking to help others. Author and teacher Eugene Petersen expands on life with others, writing, "Love cannot exist in isolation: away from others, love bloats into pride. Grace cannot be received privately: cut off from others, it is perverted into greed. Hope cannot develop in solitude." God's will for your life centers on keeping you connected with others, helping others, and doing life with others.

True Significance, In God's Eyes, Is Manifested in the Contribution of Your Life

True significance, in God's eyes, is manifested in the contribution of your life.

2 Corinthians 9:12 says,

> "This service that you perform is not only supplying the needs of God's people but is also overflowing in many expressions of thanks to God." (NIV)

The *service that you perform* means when you serve others, and meet the needs of people, then there is an overflow, and people on the outside are affected in a positive way. It's like the pebble in the pond, giving the ripple effect. As you help people, other lives get touched. The blessing goes out when you serve others.

Success versus Significance

Knowing the difference between *success* and *significance* will help you discern God's will for your life. The world defines success from a self-centered, selfish viewpoint. God invites us to do something with the life he has given us, to make an impact, to live for a purpose, and to live a life of significance by helping others.

God's will for your life centers on keeping you connected with others, helping others, and doing life with others.

As you walk through the fourth factor of knowing God's will, **The TEST Factor**, recognize that God's will for your life centers on helping others. If your plan helps no one, it's probably not God directing you. As you continue in **The TEST Factor**, God's will for your life, will shape your attitude, character, and decisions. Let's keeping testing!

The TEST Factor
Testing Your Decisions
Test Four: Become Like Christ

Chapter 19
Becoming Like Christ

"Your attitude should be the same as that of
Christ Jesus."
Philippians 2:5 (NIV)

If you lived in San Luis Obispo, California, you would be quite familiar with two prominent streets around which the entire downtown is built. Those streets are Higuera and Marsh. The unique thing about these pathways is that they are one-way streets. On at least a dozen occasions I have seen people turn the wrong way onto Higuera and Marsh, not realizing they are one-way. (The locals immediately know, "It's a vacationer!") Once the driver realizes his mistake, he frantically tries to get going the right direction. As you are discovering God's will for your life and making decisions, if those decisions are making you more like Christ, then you know you are heading the right direction. If they are not making you more like Christ, then stop, reverse, and quickly turn around!

God's will for your life will make you more like Christ. The truth of the matter is that any decision a person makes should cultivate an attitude like Christ's. The attitude a person has will shape their decisions, and will directly affect the direction they move in. A great, yet simple, question to ask yourself when attempting to know God's will is, "Will this make me more like Christ?"

Philippians 2:5 offers a high calling on our attitude,

"Your attitude should be the same as that of Christ Jesus." (NIV)

The word *attitude* means that it would be "in your mind" or "on the forefront of your mind—all the time."

A Christ-Like Attitude

Having a Christ-like attitude leads you into God's will for your life, and it will require sacrifices along the way. Becoming like Christ equates to sacrifice. Can you think of sacrifices that you have made with time, with your energy, with your money, and have you ever wondered, honestly, "Was it worth it?" God wants you to know that it wasn't just worth it—it counted for an eternity!

Sacrifice

God's will for your life has eternal impact. And eternity is a long time! The child you spent time with, the ministry you are serving in, the money you are giving to advance God's purposes, counts forever. Yet reality is, and make no mistake about it, it takes sacrifice. I'm talking about *full-on, lay your life down, "this really hurts!"* types of sacrifice! This is true because becoming like Christ will require sacrifice. Therefore, God's will for your life *will* require sacrifice. Always remember, sacrifice leads to great things. As the old sports motto says, *"No guts, no glory!"* Sacrificing takes guts. God's will for your life *will* take guts.

Becoming Like Christ Takes Other People

Not only will it take guts, it will take other people in your life. Becoming like Christ takes other people. Discovering God's will takes other people in your life.

Philippians 2:1-2 says,

> "¹If you have any encouragement from being <u>united with Christ</u>, if any comfort from his love, if any fellowship with the Spirit, if any tenderness and compassion, ²then make my joy complete by <u>being like-minded</u>, having the same love, <u>being one in spirit</u> and <u>purpose</u>." (NIV; underlines added for emphasis)

This passage is shouting, "You got any encouragement, you got any fellowship, you got any tenderness?!" It is basically saying, *"Show me what you've got!"* This works at so many levels. For example, being like-minded, and being of one spirit and purpose works in a marriage. If you are married and you show your spouse encouragement, comfort, fellowship (i.e. date night!), tenderness, and compassion, and both of you do that, you will experience unity, one spirit, and one purpose.

A great, yet simple, question to ask yourself when attempting to know God's will is, "Will this make me more like Christ?"

Knowing God's will and becoming like Christ will take other people speaking into your life. You may not like criticism. But what if that criticism gets you on track with God's will for your life? I welcome criticism in my life, if there are two conditions present. First, that the person critiquing me loves me; and second, that we are called to the same purpose.

I explain it this way: if God has called me to paddle a boat to a particular island (i.e. God's will for my life), and I have other people in my boat, and a person in my boat begins paddling to a different island, we start paddling against each other, and now we're in a power struggle. But, if a person trying to get to the same island (i.e. desires God's will for my life) criticizes me and shouts, "Thom, keep your elbow up, pull the paddle through the water longer, stop being a slacker—and paddle harder---you can do it!" those words are for my good. If we are going the same direction, I love criticism—it makes me better!

As you are walking out life with other people and walking out God's will for your life, you need to make sure you are all paddling to the same island! And you need a crystal clear picture of what that island looks like.

Humility

Becoming like Christ and knowing God's will for your life will take humility.

Philippians 2:3 highlights true humility and becoming like Christ, saying,

> "Do <u>nothing out of selfish ambition</u> or vain conceit, but in humility consider others better than yourselves."
> (NIV; underline added for emphasis)

When it says *selfish ambition*, that phrase means "to be absorbed by your own concerns." Knowing God's will for your life doesn't mean you don't have concerns; however, it means you are shooting for the happiness of everyone.

Philippians 2:4 continues,

"Each of you should look not only to your own interests, but also to the <u>interests of others</u>." (NIV; underline added for emphasis)

As you walk out God's will for your life, the interests of others should be on the forefront of your mind. The first thing you don't want in your mind is, "What can I get out of this!?" The first thing on your mind should be, "How can I help others?" That type of thinking and attitude is becoming like Christ.

This is exactly what Jesus modeled. He was in the form of God. If you are in the form of God you can do anything you want—and, being God, what you want is to do good toward human beings. So we see Jesus as a man choosing to think of others instead of Himself, modeling Himself after His Father, and thus giving us the greatest sacrifice of all.

Philippians 2:5-7 states,

"⁵Your attitude should be the same as that of Christ Jesus: ⁶ Who, <u>being in the form of God</u>, did not consider equality with God something to be grasped, ⁷ but made himself nothing, taking the very nature of a <u>servant</u>, being made in human likeness."
(NIV; underlines added for emphasis)

Choose to be a Servant

Jesus chose to be a servant. If we are becoming like Christ, then we will choose to be servants. God's will for your life will reflect being a servant, helping as many people as you can.

Serving others is not a type of "working your way to God." It's a grateful response to what God has done for you. It's like this: let's say you have been handed a billion dollars, but instead of blowing the whole thing on stupid things, you decide to be the servant. You're a billionaire and the greatest servant. Wouldn't it be funny, now being a billionaire, if you went into your work place and you just start helping out everywhere. In fact, you'd get voted the "All-Star Worker Award!" Then, someone says to you, "Wow, what happened to you? You get a bonus?" Your response would be, "You have NO idea." Knowing God's will for your life is better than a billion dollars. As a grateful response, step into servanthood.

Obedience

Knowing God's will and becoming like Christ means having great obedience.

Philippians 1:8 points out,

> "And being found in appearance as a man,
> he humbled himself and became obedient to
> death—<u>even death on a cross!</u>"
> (NIV; underline added for emphasis)

This means Jesus yielded perfect obedience. It says, "...even death on a cross." This means not only a brutal death, but one that was demoralizing and the ultimate humiliation.

Serving others is a grateful response to what God has done for you.

Sometimes obedience can seem demoralizing, yet remember, it's not. Or to other people it may seem humiliating but it is not demeaning in God's eyes.

Can you remember as a kid saying, "I don't want to obey!"? I had a childhood buddy who was fiery at best and always pressing the boundary lines. When he would get a good old-fashioned spanking, he would turn and look at his Mom and say, "That felt good!" Do you ever try to take God on that way? "That felt good... that's all You got?!"

Remember, God's Word says,

> "He disciplines those He loves."
> (Hebrews 12:6; NIV)

The reality is, God loves it when you obey! Just remember this as you are walking out God's will for your life and becoming like Christ, "after the *testing*—comes the *blessing!*" Becoming like Christ means great servanthood, great obedience, and going after God's goal for your life.

God Is Calling You to Become Like Christ

Philippians 3:14 says,

> "I press on <u>toward the goal</u> to win the prize for which God has called me heavenward <u>in Christ Jesus</u>."
> (NIV; underlines added for emphasis)

There is a goal God is calling you toward, and He is calling you to become like Christ. Ask yourself, "Is the decision I am about to make drawing me closer to Christ or pushing me away from Christ?"

As you pursue God's will for your life, remember that every decision you make in life is like building a jig-saw puzzle. You will see the picture of the puzzle come into view as you become more like Christ.

> Becoming like Christ means great servanthood, great obedience, and going after God's goal for your life.

There are two questions you can ask yourself to keep you centered in becoming like Christ and knowing God's will. First, "Who am I?" And second, "Where am I going?" Matt Damon, in *The Bourne Identity*, plays a CIA agent with amnesia. He doesn't know who he is so he hitches a ride and winds up in the Swiss Alps. He confesses to his traveling companion, Marie, "I don't know who I am or where I'm going." How absolutely horrifically frustrating that would be.

Tragically, many people are living their lives not knowing who they are or where they are going. When our true identity is in becoming like Christ, it reveals God's will for our lives. When we find out God's will for our lives, there is abundant life, real joy, deep purpose, and stabilizing peace. This leads us to the fifth and final test, "Is there peace?"

Factor Four:
The TEST Factor
Testing Your Decisions
Test Five: Feel the Peace of God

Chapter 20
Feeling the Peace of God

"And the <u>peace of God</u>, which transcends all understanding, will guard your hearts and your minds in Christ Jesus." Philippians 4:7 (NIV)

Let's say you have hit all four on the checklist of **The TEST Factor**: You see God's will for your life lining up with His word, it matches your gifts, it will help others, and it makes you more like Christ. But then you just don't have the peace of God about the decision—then, wait until you do! God uses His peace to guard your heart and your mind, and that is where you are going to discern God's will for your life. Discovering God's will takes your heart and mind. His peace will guard your inner person, so that you have the ability, even the freedom, to know His will for your life.

God's Peace on the Inside

No one really knows the source of this story, but you may have heard about the guy who had a heart attack and after he recovered he went to see the doctor? After the doctor ran tests and checked him out he called him into his office to give the prognosis. The man was so nervous he sent his wife in to get the news. The doctor sat the wife down and said, "Here is the prognosis for your husband... if you cook him three meals a day, massage his back often, and have sex every night—he's going to live." She walked out of the office and the husband asked, "Well, what did he say?" The wife replied, "He said you're going to die." Let's just say that the wife was not feeling the peace of God about that prognosis!

Seriously, if you don't have God's peace on the inside, then wait. There can be certain things that are undermining your ability to feel the peace of God. In other words, God's will for you could be very clear, yet things like fear, confusion, and even stress can cloud your peace as you attempt to discern God's will. If you have fears, ask God to take your fears. He does that by filling your heart with His perfect love. If you are battling with confusion, ask God for wisdom, the one prayer God always loves to answer.

> Discovering God's will takes your heart and mind.

The Effects of Stress

When walking through **The TEST Factor** of feeling God's peace, stress can prevent us from discerning accurately. So many things can stress us out and steal our peace: the unexpected bill, an uncertain economy, battling health issues, the challenge of relationships and parenting.

Have you ever had a day start off so stressful that it would be impossible to discern God's will? Years ago I was taking my two oldest girls to school when they were really little. It had rained hard the night before. As I pulled up to the school, the gutter by the sidewalk was raging with water. I had an old Ford Bronco and as I opened the door one of my girls literally fell out and dropped about 2-3 feet, landing in the gutter, which was about 12 inches deep in water.

I basically baptized my daughter in the gutter! She was screaming and crying, as my other daughter was standing there wondering what in the world we were doing. My daughter was sobbing, soaking, and I'm now late for work. I put them both in the car, drove home, and started all over... take two! Events happen that can stress us out so much that it will be very challenging to feel God's peace about the decision you are making. Let the dust settle before looking to feel God's peace about your decision.

Let His Peace Rule in Your Heart

God's peace is a powerful resource. Colossians 3:15 says,

> "And let the <u>peace that comes from Christ rule</u> in your hearts."
> (NIV; underline added for emphasis)

Knowing God's will for your life means getting to know Jesus Christ in a very personal way. The more you know Jesus, the more His peace will rule in your heart. The more His peace is ruling in your heart, the more you will get to know God's will.

God Keeps a Different Record of Past Mistakes

Another major hurdle that robs people of God's peace ruling in their hearts is when you focus on your past mistakes. Perhaps you have made poor decisions in the past that make you feel like, "How could I know God's will when I have these records of wrongs?" God keeps a different record. There is a dad who has a son that is autistic. He was taking his son through the typical bedtime routine. As he does every evening, he kissed him goodnight. The boy immediately sat up in bed and declared, "We need a record of kisses!" As his son said this, a scripture whispered in his memory, 1 Corinthians 13, "Love keeps no record of wrongs." (NIV) He thought of this truth: love does not keep a record of wrongs; rather, love keeps a record of kisses.

Experience Peace

When you ask for God's forgiveness, you are forgiven and there is no record of wrongs. This will free you to experience unbelievable peace. Combine this reality of God's forgiveness with the passage of Colossians 3:15 that calls us to let the peace of Christ "rule" in our hearts, and you will begin to experience peace of another kind.

This word *rule* that is used in Colossians 3:15, is like an umpire who is calling the shots in your heart, in the core of who you are. While in college I was a baseball umpire for a summer job. The head umpire told me the secret of umpires, "When you make a call 'safe' or 'out'... shout it out with such confidence and authority that every person in the ballpark believes you. You may not even make the right call; it doesn't matter, shout it like you did make the right call!" Umpires have a lot of authority to make the calls. Colossians 3:15 is saying let the peace of Christ "make the call;" that is, to umpire, rule, govern, or preside over your heart so that no matter what happens to you in life, your peace is not robbed.

The New Testament Greek word for *rule* was commonly used in reference to the Olympics and other games. It means *to be a director of the public games or sporting event, and to preside over them and preserve order, and then bestow the prizes to the victors.* The meaning here is that the peace which God gives to the soul is to be to us what the director or governor at the games was to those who competed there. God's peace is to preside over and govern the mind, and to preserve what is good, right, and true. When God's peace shines in our hearts, it saves us from the turmoil, chaos, disorder, and the crazy things that happen in life.

As you *test* your discernment of God's will for your life, the peace of Jesus needs to rule in your heart. There are certain disciplines that will empower you to feel that peace and discern correctly that include submitting, thankfulness, the Word, worship, and dedication.

> Knowing God's will for your life means getting to know Jesus Christ in a very personal way.

Submitting to Christ

If Christ and His peace are ruling over your heart, that means submitting to His rule. If you are running from Him, rebelling against Him, or ignoring Him, you will not be experiencing the peace that He offers. Did you know that submitting and obeying is simply agreeing? It's saying, "Jesus, I agree with you."

You have to let Him be your umpire. When He says, "You're OUT!" you agree and don't kick dirt at Him! When He says, "You're SAFE," you gladly accept. Here's the truth—something is ruling your heart. What is it for you? It could be fear, it could be pain, it could be sin, it could be guilt; it could be a lot of things. Submitting to Christ will help you feel God's peace when discerning His will for your life.

Thankfulness

Being a thankful person cultivates peace in your life. I have never found a thankful person who was unhappy or a happy person who wasn't thankful.

There can be really tough things going on in your life, yet there are always things to be thankful for. Every heartbeat is a gift, every breath is a gift, and if your heart is in Christ— you have an eternity of joy that awaits you in a place where there is no pain, no hurt, or tears. Thankfulness fosters the ability to feel God's peace when finding His will.

> I have never found a thankful person who was unhappy or a happy person who wasn't thankful.

The Word

Colossians 3:16 says,

"Let the word of Christ <u>dwell</u> in you richly..." (NIV; underline added for emphasis)

Having the Word dwell in you richly is taking the teaching of Jesus and letting that soak deep into your heart, taking the wisdom of His words and having them be the source, the well from which you draw.

To *dwell in you richly* is to have His Word ooze out of you—like when a person eats a lot of garlic and the garlic oozes out of their pores and everyone knows, "Somebody had garlic!" In the same way, we need to get Christ's Words deep in us, so that His wisdom oozes out of our lives. The Word in you will empower you to feel God's peace as you make decisions in your life.

Worship

Worshipping God fosters peace very quickly. It's difficult to stay stressed while worshipping the Lord. There is a powerful dynamic that happens when singing spiritual songs. When you sing the truth about God, it reinforces what you believe—it gets truth and peace resonating on the inside. It fills up your soul.

Though many times when we are stressed, the last thing we want to do is worship God. Worshipping God is like shifting the wind in a ship's sail—it sends you a different direction. Worship God and it will send you a different direction away from stress. It will foster the peace to test God's will.

Dedication

Colossians 3:17 tells us,

> "And whatever you do, whether in word or deed, do it all in the name of the Lord Jesus, giving thanks to God the Father through him." (NIV)

Whatever you do means, literally, "whatever you do!" Whether it is a spiritual activity or a temporal activity, whether the words you use or the actions you take, whether going to work or going to play golf, live dedicated to the Lord. It's a life that says, "Whatever I do—I am dedicating what I do to the Lord." And that fosters peace.

I love the movie *Chariots of Fire*, the true story of Olympic Champion, Eric Liddell. The greatest line in the movie is when Eric confesses, *"The Lord made me fast and when I run I feel His pleasure."* *Dedicating what I do to the Lord* also means doing what God made you to do, and doing it for Him!

Proverbs 16:3 says,

> "Commit to the LORD whatever you do,
> and your plans will succeed." (NIV)

I see the word *commit* in this passage like a person transferring a burden from his own back to someone else who is stronger, who is better able to bear it. Testing God's will for your life means committing it to Him. It means to transfer the burden to Him and trust in Him, which will give you peace.

Romans 15:13 declares,

> "May the God of hope fill you with all joy
> and peace <u>as you trust in him</u>, so that you may
> overflow with hope by the power of the Holy
> Spirit." (NIV; underline added for emphasis)

The key to feeling God's peace goes hand in hand with *trust*. When you trust, the natural overflow, even the supernatural overflow, is hope and power and the Holy Spirit bubbling out of your life as you walk out God's will for your life.

Having the Right Priorities

Feeling God's peace about God's will for your life is all about having the right priorities.

Colossians 3:23 says,

> "Whatever you do, work at it with all your heart, as working for the Lord, not for men." (NIV)

Shaun Alexander, who was a running back for the Seattle Seahawks and the Most Valuable Player for the 2005 NFL season, said the following in an interview, "I am a Christian that loves the Lord, that just happens to play football, that happens to get to be on cool TV shows, that happens to get to be on commercials. I'm a godly man first. I chase after God. I play football for the sole reason to give God glory." It was God's will for Shaun to play football, but Shaun's priority was to play for the Lord.

When you think you have an answer from God, test it! After testing it, throw out the bad and hold on to the good. Or in other words, eat the chicken and throw out the bones. The next time you are making a major life decision, run it through the five item checklist, and you will discover God's will for your life.

Factor Four: The TEST Factor—Testing Your Decisions
Test One: Lining up with God's Word
Test Two: Matching Your Gifts
Test Three: Helping Others
Test Four: Becoming Like Christ
Test Five: Feeling the Peace of God

We now begin to complete our journey of "How to Know God's Will" as we enter into the fifth and final factor. This gets personal, yet it's absolutely vital. The fifth factor is **The PERSONAL Factor.** Fasten your seatbelt, we now are descending and getting ready to land.

Factor Five:
The PERSONAL Factor
Following God's Will for Your Life
Walking It Out: A Life of Purity

"...if you hear his voice, do not harden your hearts."
Hebrews 4:7 (NIV)

Chapter 21
A Life of Purity

"Create in me a pure heart, O God."
Psalm 51:10 (NIV)

I teach a class where I will ask the attendees the million-dollar question, "We become what we are _____ to." Every so often someone will get the right answer to the "blank." The answer I'm looking for is the word *committed*.

My point is that the biggies in life do not naturally happen. If I want to become a great husband, I have to *commit* to being a great husband; it won't occur by happenstance. If I want to become a great father, I have to *commit* to being a great father; no magic wand will say, "Poof, you're a great dad!" The really important things in life require extremely hard work and do not naturally happen on their own.

Living a life of purity is on the list of biggies. You have to commit to it. A life of purity won't just happen, yet it is critical to walking out God's will for your life.

A Life of Purity Does *Not* Mean Perfection

It is also vital to understand that a life of purity does *not* mean perfection. It does *not* mean that one day you will arrive into a perfect state where you never make a mistake again. No one is perfect and everybody makes mistakes; that is what it means to be human. At the same time pursuing a life of purity is absolutely needed in arriving to God's will for your life. Anyone can get God's message and calling, yet miss out on His best because of living outside of what God already says is good, right, and true.

The opposite of something being pure is tainted. Our lives can get tainted. And just a little tainting still can cloud the whole picture. If I offered you a glass of water with just a pinch of dirt in it, you would not be so thrilled about drinking my water. Better yet, if I gave you a glass of water with just a "smidge" of arsenic, you would have me locked up! We can have just a little bit of taint in our lives that muddies the waters just enough to the point where we can't effectively and clearly walk out God's will for our lives.

Part of living a life of purity simply means taking an inventory of our lives and chucking the junk out the door!

That's what Hebrews 12:1 encourages us to do when it says,

> "Therefore, since we are surrounded by such a great cloud of witnesses, let us <u>throw off</u> <u>everything</u> that hinders and the sin that so easily entangles."
> (NIV; underline added for emphasis)

> A life of purity won't just happen,
> yet it is critical to walking out God's will for your life.

Sin Messes Up a Person's Life

The topic of *sin* really is a no brainer. Sin messes up a person's life. God loves you so much that He gives you boundary lines to live within. When you go outside those lines, it causes all kinds of problems in life. So scripture instructs us to throw off everything that hinders us from walking out God's will. It is different for everyone. What has you entangled will be different than what entangles other people. The list of entanglements may include doubt, arrogance, worry, lust, fear, greed, or hatred, to name a few.

When I consider the scripture that says *the sin that so easily entangles*, I immediately think of my fish line when I have attempted to take my kids fishing over the years. My fishing line inevitably gets caught on something and snagged. I (sadly) typically begin to pull and tug, and before I'm through I have created a ball of fishing line so ensnarled that I need to cut the line and start over! It's embarrassing, but it's the truth.

Sin wraps us up in knots where we can't function correctly. The good news is that God's grace lets us cut the line and start afresh. Our part needs to be a willingness to cut the line, to throw off anything that is hindering us from God's best.

> ...pursuing a life of purity is absolutely needed in arriving to God's will for your life.

A Good Offense for Living a Life of Purity

Throwing off the entanglements of life is a good defense. What makes for a good offense for living a life of purity? There are three things that you can pursue that will cultivate a life of purity. In the game of basketball there is the "three-point shot." It is when a player shoots the ball from outside a painted arc and if the player makes it, the team gets three points for the made basket instead of the normal two points. A lot of teams will live and die by the three point shot. If they shoot and make a lot of three point shots they win, and if they miss a lot of three point shots they usually lose.

When attempting to live a life of purity, it is also true that we will live and die by three points: a pure heart, a good conscience, and a sincere faith. These three points help us win at living pure.

In 1 Timothy 1:5 we read,

> "Now the purpose of the commandment is love from a pure heart, from a good conscience, and from sincere faith." (NIV)

God wants you to have a three point offense for life: a pure heart, good conscience, and sincere faith. If having a pure heart, a good conscience, and a sincere faith are not happening, a person begins to die on the inside. If those three are happening in the inner life of an individual, they will live, thrive, and experience a life of purity.

Pure Heart

In chapter two we went after *preparing our hearts* to get ready to hear from God. Having a pure heart will be required to live out what God has called you to do.

Proverbs 4:23 tells us,

> "Guard your heart above all else, for it determines the course of your life." (NLT)

We have to go back to the core of who we are over and over again, because it affects every issue of our lives. We have to check our motives at the depth of our being.

You could be attempting to go after very worthy causes, yet not have a pure heart. Years ago I was interviewing a surgeon who would fly into impoverished nations and perform unbelievable surgeries on little children. During the interview, I asked, "Why do you do what you do?" He swiftly responded, "Because it makes me feel like God... but don't print that!" My heart sunk into my gut. I didn't know whether to laugh or cry; I mostly felt like crying, as I was sick to my stomach. He was doing wonderful acts of service, kindness, and compassion, yet his heart was tainted with arrogance—motivated by power and the desire to feel like God. His impure heart had him missing out on something better.

Good Conscience

Having a "good conscience" is having a "clear conscience." Every one of us can think back on the wrongs we've done and the wrongs that have been done to us. We can carry around the guilt, shame, and stains of life. God wants to wash away our stains! He desires for us to have a clear conscience.

That's why He tells us in 1 John 1:9,

"If we confess our sins, he is faithful and just and will forgive us our sins and purify us from all unrighteousness." (NIV)

Once you have received Christ's offer of forgiveness and purifying, then the stains have been removed. There is no need to point them out again. Every pair of pants I have ever owned eventually gets baptized in spilt coffee. I have stained more pants then I'd like to confess to. I have even had the pants professionally cleaned and the stains were absolutely removed. Bringing up the things that God has forgiven and the stains He has purified is like purposely pouring coffee back on your pants where the stain was!

Living a life of purity is allowing Christ to purify you, and that creates a good conscience within. Continue to focus on cultivating a pure heart and a good conscience, which will empower you to fulfill God's will for your life.

Sincere Faith

Having a sincere faith simply means being genuine, versus being hollow or self-serving. When you are being genuine with a sincere faith, you will be walking out God's will with integrity. You will be living a life of purity.

Living a pure life has so much to do with what is going on in the inside of you. The person who commits adultery did not just wake up one morning and say, "I'm going to go out and commit adultery today!" That is not how it happens. The person tragically thought about it for days, weeks, even months before it occurred. A friend of mine told me the story of meeting with someone who had such a failure. The downcast guy, who had failed, shook his head and said, *"I don't know how this could have happened."* My friend immediately responded, *"Yes you do. You thought about it for months before it happened."* The man broke down sobbing, crying, *"You're right... you're right."*

> Living a pure life has so much to do with what is going on in the inside of you.

Living a pure life is worth it. Focusing on having a *pure heart, a good conscience, and a sincere faith* will set someone up for success. Tainting one's life with thoughts and desires contrary to God's goodness will set that person up for disaster and heartache.

Will we always be perfect and never make mistakes? No. God is like a potter. He gets his hands dirty working in our mud, but His goal is our purity. That's why He is a God of second chances. He is not afraid to work in the muck and mire of our lives to bring about His will.

No matter what you have done, you must understand that God is a God of mercy. He works with you, in the midst of the mud of your life. Let Christ cleanse you, and then don't give up on committing to purity—it will lead you to walking out God's will for your life.

The next chapter is all about "not giving up." Walking out God's will for your life will require perseverance. Don't give up—read on!

> No matter what you have done,
> there is a God of second chances.

Factor Five:
The PERSONAL Factor
Following God's Will for Your Life
Walking It Out: A Life of Perseverance

Chapter 22
A Life of Perseverance

"You need to persevere so that when you have done the will of God, you will receive what he has promised."
Hebrews 10:36
(NIV; underlines added for emphasis)

Perseverance does not mean you won't get knocked down in life--it does mean you get back up after the knock down, or setback, or failure. Perseverance does not mean that you will be perfect. Perseverance means when you fall, you will get back up for the race.

Proverbs 24:16 says,

> "It's the righteous person who falls seven times, but gets back up all seven times." (NIV)

Perseverance: When You Fall, You Get Back Up

When I was in college I trained for a triathlon. I had never done one before and so the whole thing was a new experience for me. I had a good friend that had competed in a handful of triathlons, so he was coaching me. The day of the race I woke up and headed to a fast food place for breakfast. I was young and dumb, therefore I never scarfed down so much fast food. If it was food and it was fast, then I ate it! I got back to the house and my friend/coach is standing on the porch. With a glare in his eye, he asked, "Where did you go?" I mumbled out the words like a little boy caught with his hand in the cookie jar, "A fast food place." He quickly responded, "What'd you have to eat?" After I confessed of the amount of fast food I had absorbed, He could not believe it. My friend/coach then instructed me,

"You better get rid of it now, or you'll definitely get rid of it later!" After his disgust of my fast food eating spree, he said, "Okay, get on the bike and warm up a little bit." So I locked my feet into the pedals of the bike, slowly headed down the street, and began to gradually warm up. I decided to turn around and go back to the house, turning into a cul-de-sac. Little did I know, the city had just poured gravel on the pavement to resurface the road. As I turned the bike around, the thin tires lost all control on the gravel and the bike totally slid out from under me with my feet locked in the pedals! It was not pretty. I scraped my skin from my hip to my ankle. Scene two... I come hobbling into the house, bleeding, gravel imbedded in my skin, and all my friend/coach could say was, "UGLY." Then I went out and competed in the triathlon race with a fast food gut bulging, skin bleeding, and pride demolished.

Okay, I learned two critical things about perseverance and about Proverbs' encouragement to get back up.

1. Sometimes we make individual decisions that are stupid! Decisions like scarfing down fast food on the day of a triathlon are flat out dumb. However, despite the stupid decisions, we still need to persevere and get back up in the race.

2. Sometimes things happen to us that we have no control over. Circumstances can come our way, like the gravel that made my bike crash. Yet, we have to persevere and get back up in the race even when things happen to us. We have to persevere in light of the wrongs we have done and the wrongs done to us.

In life, you will potentially make stupid decisions, and in life there will be people who do you wrong. God calls you to persevere anyway. He calls you to get back up and walk out His will for your life.

Hebrews 12:1 shouts,

"...let us <u>run with perseverance</u>."
(NIV; underline added for emphasis)

The writer of this ancient truth calls us to persevere and live a life of perseverance. The Bible often refers to life as a race, or a run, and just like a competitive runner perseveres, so we must in the race of life—as we walk out God's will.

Hebrews 10:36 gives a high calling to living out God's will,

"<u>You need to persevere</u> so that when you have done the <u>will of God</u>, you will receive what he has promised."

(NIV; underlines added for emphasis)

God says the reason why you need to persevere is to do His will. When we do God's will there is a reward, a promise. Notice that scripture says that you receive something when you persevere. What you receive is an eternal promise that includes a mansion in the sky, streets paved with gold, and life with God forever and ever... but wait there's more... the peace of God and favor of God while living here on earth.

Yet, life is not always easy and walking out God's will is not always easy. There are certain things that can happen in our lives that make us want to quit, and in this case quit on God's perfect and pleasing will for our lives. Scripture points to three things that put up a fight to a life of perseverance, which include stress, failures, and tiredness.

Stress that Results in Overwhelming Pressure

The Apostle Paul, who penned the majority of the New Testament, becomes very transparent when he shares in 2 Corinthians 1:8,

"We were under great pressure, far beyond
our ability to endure, so that we despaired
even of life." (NIV)

He was being honest that there was so much stress
happening that it impaired his ability to endure and he
didn't want to keep living life. Paul goes on to say in his
heart he felt a "sentence of death." It really doesn't get more
depressing than that. However, he came to the conclusion
that he could not rely on himself, yet could only rely on God
to see him through. In fact his whole perspective changed
when he looked at the stress he was enduring was allowed
in his life so that he would rely on God.

Back in 1999 God had put in my heart the call to lead our
church to our very first property, a place that we could call
home and that would facilitate tons of ministry for years to
come. God led us to a beautiful piece of acreage overlooking
the city, and we went into escrow in June of 1999. Then the
stress began! There was financial pressure as oil prices
skyrocketed, affecting building costs. There was some
political pressure from certain city officials when I was told
behind closed doors, "This project will never happen."
(Let's just say that my heart was not encouraged after those
types of meetings.) Then there was the reality of the stress in
attempting to help people catch the vision of what God

wanted to do on that land. I had people leave the church over the issue which again was very painful for me. Truth be known, there were times that I felt overwhelmed, wanting to quit. However, I knew God had called me to complete His good and perfect will. After persevering for almost ten years after going into escrow, we moved into our new facility that sits on 63 acres that blesses thousands of people on the Central Coast of California.

Don't let stress overwhelm you to the place where you quit on what God has placed in your heart. Just know that not quitting will require living a life of perseverance.

Failures that Result In Personal Disappointment

Luke 22:60-62 tells the story of Peter denying Christ. This was a defining moment in his life that could have knocked him out of the race for good.

Scripture says,

> "Peter replied, '[60]Man, I don't know what you're talking about!' Just as he was speaking, the rooster crowed. [61] The Lord turned and looked straight at Peter. Then Peter re-membered the word the Lord had spoken to

him: 'Before the rooster crows today, you will disown me three times.' [62] And he went outside and wept bitterly." (NIV)

This was a devastating failure in Peter's life, and it brings a whole new understanding to the phrase, "For Pete's sake!" Peter was so personally disappointed that he wept from the gut in an uncontrollable manner.

I know that when I have failed there is the temptation to quit. When I say the wrong thing that hurts others, or think the wrong thing that does not honor God, there is a deep, deep sense of disappointment. Any one of us can get caught in a moment where we lash out. One morning I was looking for some quiet time, wanting to snuggle up on the couch with a cup of hot coffee and listen to my radio teaching program. My moment of solitude was being swiftly interrupted as two of my kids were arguing and yelling in the background. The noise kept escalating, and in that moment my voice comes on the radio and says, "Do you want to be a better parent? Stay tuned." I looked at the radio and seriously said, "Oh, shut up!" Now, you know you've lost it when you yell at yourself to shut up!

When you have moments of failures, don't allow the disappointment to make you quit on walking out God's will for your life. Peter, who denied Christ, came back to lead the church, pen scripture, and live out a miraculous ministry. Grieve your failures, turn from them, receive Christ's grace, and run after God's will for your life! If Peter could do that, so can you.

Tiredness that Results in Physical, Emotional, and Spiritual Exhaustion

David of the Old Testament is a fiery character. As a boy he conquers an intimidating giant, he later becomes a king, and worships God with such zeal that he was known to dance before the Lord in pretty much his underwear! David oozed with passion. Whether he was fighting for justice or pursuing God, he would lay it all on the line.

At the same time he was quite poetic and musical. And in a moment of honesty, he cries out in Psalm 38:10,

> "My heart pounds, my strength fails me;
> even the light has gone from my eyes." (NIV)

In this moment of his life, David was worn out. He was done in physically, emotionally, and spiritually. Yet, he also acknowledged that God was the strength of his heart and his portion forever. The bottom line is we all have seasons in our life where we are just plain old tired. (Can I get an "Amen!"?)

When my wife and I were married for about five years and we had a toddler and a baby we were absolutely drained—exhausted beyond compare. I was running a small business, writing for companies, and she was raising our first two daughters. Our first daughter was the perfect baby, sleeping through the night at four weeks old. Then came number two child, who was a bit colicky, and when she was upset (i.e. hungry, poopy diaper, etc.) she would make sure you knew. When the attention shifted to our needy baby, our firstborn hit the "terrible two's." It was a sweet season in some ways, and absolutely exhausting at the same time. During this crazy season of life, my wife and I happen to stumble onto a Christian parenting program on the radio. When the expert said to us, "And if you have a toddler and a baby at the same time this is the most physically, emotionally, and spiritually draining season of your life." My wife and I looked at each other and starting crying, "We're normal… we're normal!"

Let me encourage you. You may find yourself in a very fast paced time in your life. These are the times of life that I like to call "seasons of intensity." If you are drained, tired, and worn out, just know that "this too shall pass." If you are tired, persevering actually means getting some rest.

Whether you are physically, emotionally, or spiritually pooped out, draw back and fight for some down time. God wants you to finish the race you have been called to. He wants you to fulfill His will for your life. Let me suggest some ways to persist when you are stressed out, struggling through past failures, or so tired you are ready to quit.

Recall Your Vision

Eugene H. Peterson paraphrases the words of Jesus in Matthew 11:28 so well when he writes,

> "Are you tired? Worn out? Burned out on religion? Come to me." (*The Message*)

When we are burnt out we need to come to the Lord and be reminded of the original instructions, the first call, the vision that was painted.

Try to remember the words of Habakkuk 2:3,

> "Slowly, steadily, surely, the time approaches when the vision will be fulfilled. If it seems slow, wait patiently, for it will surely take place. It will not be delayed." (NLT)

This is a great reminder that God has perfect timing. We have to recall the vision and then wait for it. The fact that the "vision" will not be delayed means that God will see it through at the perfect time. And I have discovered that my timing is not always God's timing. He is never too early and He is never too late. He is on time, all the time, according to "His" time.

Renew Your Hope

Renewing our hope means you have to remind yourself of what is true. There is a wonderful reminder of hope found in the New Testament when Romans 5:2-5 states,

> "And we rejoice in the hope of the glory of God. [3] Not only so, but we also rejoice in our sufferings, because we know that suffering produces perseverance; [4] perseverance, character; and character, hope. [5] And hope does not disappoint us, because God has poured out his love into our hearts by the Holy Spirit, whom he has given us." (NIV)

Hope is what keeps us moving forward in life, come what may. I was on a very long "fun" run. It was a race to the top of a mountain and then back down again—if you can call that fun. The toughest part for me was the last leg of getting to the top of the mountain. I figured I could just put myself in neutral and coast down the mountain. Toward the tail of going up the mountain, prior to reaching the top, the running trail began to traverse back and forth. I felt like quitting and was gasping for air. I looked up and caught a glimpse of the top of the mountain. That was all I needed. I got a taste of the destination. It offered hope to a weary traveler. It was just what I needed to keep persevering and reach the top.

If you find yourself full of despair, I want to encourage you to renew your hope. Believe that with God all things are possible. Renewing our hope is the key ingredient to living a life of perseverance.

Replenish Your Soul

Jesus says in Matthew 11:28,

> "I'll show you how to take a real rest."
> (*The Message*)

David in the Old Testament masterfully pens Psalm 23. Psalm 23 is so popular—I even saw it used in a Nike commercial.

David writes,

> "The LORD is my shepherd, I shall not be in want. ² He makes me lie down in green pastures, he leads me beside quiet waters, ³ he restores my soul." (Psalm 23:1-3; NIV)

David knew that the Lord had the ability to restore his soul, to replenish his inner-life. This is critical in living a life of perseverance.

Psalm 42 has the Psalmist actually giving his soul instructions!

> "Why are you downcast, O my soul? Why so disturbed within me? Put your hope in God, for I will yet praise him, my Savior and my God. My soul is downcast within me; therefore I will remember you."
> (Psalm 42:5-6; NIV)

Notice the key is to put your hope in God.

Recommit Your Vow

Part of living a life of perseverance and walking out God's will for your life is recommitting your vow to God.

While King Solomon was reflecting on life, he penned in Ecclesiastes 5:4,

> "So when you make a promise to God, don't delay in following through, for God takes no pleasure in fools. Keep all the promises you make to him." (NLT)

There have been times in my life where I literally have gone back to God and said, "I'm keeping my promise." Though sometimes we need to be reminded. I was dropping my son off to school when he was about eight years old. As he began to get out of the car as I was dropping him off, I said to him, "Be a good boy." He turned to me and without blinking an eye fired back, "Okay, be a good man!" I thought, "Okay, Lord, when my son is keeping me accountable, I need to step up and recommit my vow to You."

Receive the Rhythm of Grace

Coming back to Eugene Peterson's paraphrase, my favorite verse that he articulates so well is Matthew 11:30,

> "Learn the unforced rhythms of grace. I won't lay anything heavy or ill-fitting on you.

Keep company with me and you'll learn to live feely and lightly." (*The Message*)

The rhythm of grace is a life that is filled with the love of God. It flows gently and powerfully all at the same time. It understands the true meaning of grace and results in a life given to God. We can't work our way to God, but everything we do for Him is grateful response because of His grace.

Hebrews 13:9 puts it best,

"It is good for our hearts to be strengthened by grace." (NIV)

One application of *grace* is *the power to do what God has called you to do*. A life of perseverance is filled with that kind of grace. It's available to all who would ask.

Whether you are physically, emotionally, or spiritually pooped out, draw back and fight for some down time. God wants you to finish the race you have been called to. He wants you to fulfill His will for your life.

As you are walking out God's will for your life, it will require a kind of perseverance where you must remind yourself of what God said. Adam and Eve were tricked into eating the forbidden fruit because Satan essentially said to them, "Did God say? Did God say?" Adam and Eve began to doubt, and eventually caved in. The devil still uses the same lies, and you will have thoughts that challenge what God has revealed to you. When those doubts shoot through your mind, "Did God really say that?" remind yourself of Factor Four—**The TEST Factor**. Persevere through the doubt and regain your focus on the purposes that God has called you to. That's the next thing that we need to zoom in on to walk out God's will... a life of pursuing God's purposes.

Factor Five:
The PERSONAL Factor
Following God's Will for Your Life
Walking It Out: A Life of Pursuing God's Purposes

Chapter 23
A Life of Pursuing God's Purposes

"Let us run with perseverance the race marked out for us."
Hebrews 12:1 (NIV)

God has a race just for you. One of my daily prayers is, "God, help me to run the race marked out for me." I don't want to run someone else's race; I want the one marked out for me!

Years ago when I was in my early 30's, I was reading the autobiography of Billy Graham. As he explained his life journey he mentioned that by age 30 he had met with the President of the United States, and continued to meet thereafter with each reigning president. I leaned over to my wife in astonishment and said, "Billy Graham was meeting with the President of the United States at age 30. I haven't even met with the mayor yet!" She turned to me and graciously said, "Well, you're not Billy Graham, now are you." I wasn't sure if she was picking a fight or telling the truth, as I gave her "the look." Then it quickly dawned on me that she was telling the truth! God wants me to run my race, and if that means that someday He needs me to meet with the U.S. President, then so be it. Yet the truth is my race isn't Billy's race, or anyone else's for that matter. When Hebrews 12:1 tells us, *"...the race marked out for us..."* that really means God has a race picked out just for you, and that is His purpose you need to pursue... for the rest of your life.

As you run that race, pursuing that life purpose, there is something that God calls all people to. Remember that God has a *specific* will and a *general* will. The specific will is unique to each person, and His general will is what He calls all believers to.

> God has a race picked out just for you,
> and that is His purpose you need to pursue...
> for the rest of your life.

God's Purpose: To Love Him with All You've Got

Let's review God's general will. I was in a church leadership meeting and had handed out three-by-five cards for people to ask me questions. One of the cards that came back to me said, *"What is the meaning of life?"* In that moment I wasn't sure if the person who wrote that question was trying to be funny, testing my answer, or genuinely desired direction. So I pointed the question back to what Jesus said was the most important thing in life, reciting His words in Mark 12:30, 31 (NIV):

> "[30]'The most important one,' answered Jesus, 'is this...Love the Lord your God with all your heart and with all your soul and with all your mind and with all your strength. [31] The second is this: Love your neighbor as yourself. There is no commandment greater than these.'"

In three brief sentences, Jesus had the canny ability to summarize the entire Old Testament into a great commandment. Jesus' opening statement of *"The most important one..."* is more significant than what you might think. When the teacher of the Old Testament law made a reference to "the commandments," it was focused on a popular debate about the *more important* and *less important* of the hundreds of laws that had been accumulated. The Pharisees, who vigorously studied the laws, had classified over 600 laws and spent much time discussing which laws were weightier than others. So Jesus boils it all down, takes the entire Old Testament and summarizes God's *general* will for all people in a single sentence... *"Love God with everything you've got, and love your neighbor the way you want to be loved."* So that became my answer to the "meaning of life" question: "Love God and love people."

God's purpose for all people is to love Him with all our heart, mind, soul and strength. A life of pursuing God's purpose will forever involve loving Him with the core of your being. Your heart is the throne of desire and the most important thing you could do is desire God. Think of the things that you could desire in a given week: chocolate, a great movie with popcorn, a big steak, a good work out, a great conversation with a loved one, **chocolate**... (*Sorry, I already said that one.*)

We were created to desire and it all started when we were babies. I call it the "Wahhh" factor, as in a baby's cry, *"Wahhh—where's my milk!"* And then as we grow, the "Wahhh" factor just changes its focus to other things, like sports, relationships, and cars, to whatever. God made us to desire God first and foremost, and when we do this, everything comes into alignment. In that moment life makes sense. No matter how unique God's will and purpose is for your life, it always involves loving Him with everything you've got and loving *others* with everything you've got.

God's Purpose: Love Others as Yourself

Jesus also said,

> "The second is this: Love your neighbor as yourself." (Mark 12:31a; NIV)

Believe it or not, strength in God is found when we serve others. Serving others is serving God! Jesus gave us an incredible life-altering principle when he said, "Give and you will receive." When we serve others, something happens to us! As we make a difference in someone's life, we in return get energized. A life of pursuing God's purposes will always mean loving God *and* loving people. And truth be known, loving and serving other people takes an attitude of commitment, dedication, and guts.

One Sunday morning I came walking into the church, needing to teach within 30 minutes and I was sporting a bulging black eye! While driving to the service I tried to remove a grocery cart that someone had left on the lower part of the church property. So I pulled my truck over to the side of the road. As I hoisted the grocery cart into my truck, a metal bar swung out and cracked me in the eye. I felt like I was in a Jackie Chan movie, "Which one of you all kicked me?!" I walked into church that morning and one of the pastors looked at me and said, "How we doing?" (i.e. "You look like you've just been in a bar fight and lost.") Serving others can cost you, and even be painful! Yet it's an attitude of pursuit that is required. This attitude says that nothing is going to stop you from pursuing God's purposes.

To *love your neighbor as yourself* is a second and equally important purpose. This high call focuses on "horizontal" relationships—our dealings with fellow human beings. A person cannot maintain a good vertical relationship with God (loving Him) without also caring for his or her neighbor. When Jesus used the word *neighbor* it referred to fellow human beings in general. The love a person has for himself or herself (in the sense of looking out for oneself, caring about best interests, etc.) should be maintained, but it should also be directed toward others.

The Ten Commandments and all the other Old Testament laws are summarized in these two laws: love God and love people. By fulfilling these two commands to love God totally and love others as one's self, a person will keep all the other commands.

Think of the Ten Commandments:

> No other gods before God, no idols, no misusing God's name, keeping one day a week for worship, honoring your mother and father, don't murder, don't commit adultery, don't steal, don't lie, and don't covet.

If you totally love God (vertical) and totally love others (horizontal), you're NOT going to violate any of those Ten Commandments. Love becomes the guiding force. Loving God and loving people is God's will for you and His purpose for you to pursue.

Now when you are loving people, by definition *you do what is best for them.* Sometimes that takes tough love and it really is an issue of the heart. It is critical that when you are in the battle of life you are seeing and discerning accurately. It's like a boxer who is getting plummeted and can hardly see straight, his eyes are swollen, and he does whatever he can do to keep his vision intact.

Relationships can sometimes feel like the boxing ring where you just feel beat up. In that moment your eyes are not seeing straight. In that moment you have to look to the Lord and love Him. As you love Him something special begins to happen. As you love God from the heart, you begin to see straight. His love has that ability to make wrong things right. His love helps us see correctly. His love can empower you to LOVE others and that's our highest call.

> Loving God and loving people is God's will for you and His purpose for you to pursue.

God's Purpose: Running Your Unique Race

As you run the race that is picked out for you by God, loving Him and other people goes hand in hand with pursuing His unique purpose for your life. The key is to pursue God's purposes for a lifetime.

Be determined to finish the race you have been assigned so that you may echo the words of Paul's letter to a young man named Timothy, as he writes in 2 Timothy 4:7,

"I have fought the good fight. I have finished the race. I have kept the faith." (NIV)

That is a statement of a man who absolutely lived a life of pursuing God's purposes.

Sometimes we will find ourselves running a race we didn't expect to be in. The assignment is from God, yet perhaps you never imagined yourself to be on that particular path. However, I encourage you to follow the advice of my pastor when I was growing in faith. He would say, "Be a F.A.T. Christian." By that he meant, "Be faithful, available, and teachable."

When I was in high school, playing on the baseball team, the track coach had a meet where he was short a few team members, so he asked if some of us baseball players would pitch in and participate in the track meet. A buddy of mine and I jumped at the chance. At the day of the meet I asked the coach what race he picked for me to run. He said, "The 330 hurdles." (The 330 hurdles race is three-fourths of a lap with hurdles about every 30 yards.) I thought, "No problem. Every so often jump over a hurdle; heck, it's not even a full lap!" I came busting out from the start line in my newfound race, absolutely full of confidence. I was in first place after the first hurdle! Then it began to set in. After the second and third hurdle, exhaustion was overtaking me. I had never done this event in my life and immediately thought, "How did I get myself into this race!?" I felt like crawling under the last hurdle instead of jumping over it. However, I crossed the finish line and scored a point for my team.

The point is you may find yourself in a race that God has assigned you. It may be very different than what you are used to. It may be way more difficult than what you expected. Don't quit! Commit your life to finishing the race.

> The key is to pursue God's purposes for a lifetime.

From Factor One: **The YOU Factor**, you are prepared to hear from God. There is full understanding of how God speaks, which is Factor Two: **The GOD Factor**. Carefully you have listened and received an answer from God as described by Factor Three: **The GOD and YOU Factor**. Putting it to the test, the answer has cleared Factor Four: **The TEST Factor**. Finally, you are walking out God's will for your life with a life of *purity, perseverance,* and a *pursuit of God's purposes*. There are two more elements to Factor Five: **The PERSONAL Factor**... *prayer* and *passion*. These two themes are of epic proportion to fulfilling God's will. Read on, we're getting close to the finish line.

Factor Five:
The PERSONAL Factor
Following God's Will for Your Life
Walking It Out: A Life of Prayer

Chapter 24
A Life of Prayer

"Be joyful always, <u>pray continually</u>, give thanks in all circumstances; for this is <u>God's will for you</u> in Christ Jesus."
1 Thessalonians 5:16-18
(NIV; underlines for emphasis)

I have taught my church over and over again a certain prayer that is very powerful, and it's worth repeating here. I call it the "Oh God" prayer. It goes like this, "Oh God, Oh God, Oh God, Oh God, Oh God!!!" As if to say, *"Oh Lord, I really need your help and fast."* This is the prayer in a crisis moment; however, God wants us to develop a daily, lifelong, passionate life of prayer.

Three Styles of Prayer

There are really three styles of prayer and all three are equally important. Those three styles include: a daily rhythm of prayer, crisis moments of prayer, and an on-going conversation.

Daily Rhythm

Most people want to have a daily prayer life, yet it can be such a challenge. In the words of Jesus,

> "The spirit is willing, but the flesh is weak!"
> (Matthew 26:41; NIV)

Believe you me, I know the challenge of trying to carve out time in a busy schedule, or dragging myself out of bed early in the morning, or having my mind so distracted that I end up landing on a certain thought, thinking, "How in the world did I get to thinking about this?!" I call that the "domino effect." This is how it works... I'm praying for somebody in our church that has an Italian last name, and while I'm praying my mind says,

> "They're Italian... I love Italian food for dinner... I wonder what my wife, Sherri is going to make for dinner tonight... I hope she makes her secret bean dish... I wonder what kind of beans she uses?"

Where does the madness stop? I'm praying for a church member and I land on thinking about beans! You get the point—our minds wander.

Yet, the key to having a daily prayer life is finding a rhythm that works for you. And the goal is to make it daily. One of my mentors has told me over the years, "Success is to just keep showing up." We can apply that to developing a life of prayer. Just keep showing up. God sees your attempt to meet with Him. You may feel groggy, and have "bed head" in full bloom, yet the Lord delights in you just showing up.

I want to encourage you to go for quality over quantity. So many people get discouraged because they hear of people who pray for one, two, three hours a day. God bless those saints; however, not all of us are going to be able to pray for that long. I think ten minutes of passionate focused prayer everyday would be more beneficial than floundering to "clock in" a certain amount of time. Think consistency, daily, and about being transparent.

The Psalmist says,

> "Trust in him at all times, you people; pour out your hearts to him, for God is our refuge." (Psalm 62:8; NIV)

Prayer is simply talking to God and pouring your heart out to Him.

...go for quality over quantity.

Years ago I was sitting in a church service and the guest speaker was giving a message on developing a life of prayer. I was struggling at that time to maintain a daily rhythm. The pastor said, "I am going to tell you the secret in having a daily prayer life." All of a sudden I was on the edge of my seat, armed with pen in hand and yellow pad ready. I couldn't believe it. He was going to give me the "secret" of actualizing a life of prayer. The guest speaker went on to say, "And the secret to having a daily life of prayer is block out time in your daily planner." I felt so dumb. I was waiting for some lofty spiritual truth, yet the truth was plain and simple: have a set time in your daily routine.

> Prayer is simply talking to God and pouring your heart out to Him.

There is something powerful and life changing when we create good habits on a daily basis. It's been understood that if we do something for 30 days straight it will develop into a habit. Schedule in your ten minutes every day (or more if you want, but make it do-able) and begin to create a daily rhythm.

Also, remember it's more than okay to mix it up. Some people like to journal their prayers, some find it more effective to take a walk and pray, and some like to curl up on the couch with a hot cup of coffee and share their heart with the Lord. I like to mix it up, using one of those three approaches to prayer in a given season, then to switch to a different one for a season.

Crisis Moments

Back to the "Oh God" prayer... there will be moments in your life where storms quickly rage and you are absolutely desperate. In those scary times we need to call on God immediately. We need to make prayer the first action, not the last resort. Don't be the person who says, "Well, we have tried everything, I guess we should pray."

To be crystal clear, God calls us to courage and quick action. No one knows for sure where this story comes from, but perhaps you have heard about the guy who was stuck on top of his roof in the midst of a massive flood. He prayed, "Oh God, do a miracle and save me!" A guy in a boat came by and said, "Quick! Jump in my boat." The man replied, "No, thank you. I'm waiting for God to save me." Then a Coast Guard ship came up, with the speakers blasting, "Take hold of the life preserver and we will pull you into the ship." The man replied, "No, thank you. I'm waiting for God to save me." Finally, a helicopter came overhead, lowering down a ladder, with the message, "Climb up the ladder!" The man replied, "No, thank you. I'm waiting for God to save me." Well the waters rose, and the man tragically died, yet went to heaven. He immediately said to God, "Why didn't you do a miracle and save me?" The Lord replied, "What did you want? I sent you a boat, ship, and helicopter."

In crisis moments pray immediately and take the open doors as God's provision. Crisis moments call us to "pray and apply pressure." A few years ago my son was sick. He had that look on his face that *all* was not right. If that wasn't enough, his nose burst into bleeding. It was quite a moment to be holding my son, holding his nose (applying pressure like I have been taught), and feeling a bit helpless. His nose had no sign of letting up as it continued to bleed profusely. All I could do was pray and apply pressure. Isn't that life? We pray for the Lord to do something on our behalf and trust that He is in control as we apply pressure, meaning we do all that we can do.

God instructs us in Ephesians 6:13,

> "Therefore put on the full armor of God, so that when the day of evil comes, you may be able to stand your ground, and <u>after you have done everything,</u> to stand."

Then in verse 18 it says,

> "And <u>pray</u> in the Spirit on all occasions with all kinds of prayers and requests." (Both verses NIV; underlines added for emphasis)

In crisis moments we are called to do everything we can to fight the good fight and we pray like there is no tomorrow. So whatever you face, pray and apply pressure, because God calls us to both: pray and act.

An example of a prayer in crisis looks like this, "Lord, please help me in this situation and deliver me. I also pray that you would inspire me to do all I can do and trust you with the results. Amen."

> We pray for the Lord to do something on our behalf and trust that He is in control as we apply pressure, meaning we do all that we can do.

Over 20 years ago, my oldest daughter was ten months old when she came down with a horribly high fever that led us to get to the doctors immediately. I still can remember the chilling cold feeling of a doctor sitting down with my wife and me in a private room to explain that she had a rare virus and all they could do is to place her on an IV in the children's emergency room, not knowing if she would make it. We burst into tears, agonizing from the depths of our being. A couple of days went by with no sign of her temperature coming down. It seems like it was yesterday, as the crisis moment of prayer is vivid in my mind to this day. I went into the bathroom at the hospital and was staring into the mirror, yet it felt more like I was staring right through my soul. It was a bit of a spiritual gut check. I cried out to the Lord, "God, You have to do something. You're all I've got. You're the only one who can do something. Lord, I need you. Please do something." Within an hour of that prayer, her temperature began to fall and within 24 hours we were out of the hospital and back to normal.

I don't want to suggest that there is some magical prayer that absolutely moves the hand of God. It is a delicate issue, as I have close friends who have lost children to sickness. Though my friends who have endured such unimaginable horrific pain at the loss of a child would still agree that in moments of crisis, cry out to God.

In the Old Testament David models a prayer in a crisis moment in Psalm 142:1-3 that you and I could use:

> "I cry aloud to the LORD; I lift up my voice to the LORD for mercy. I pour out before him my complaint; before him I tell my trouble. When my spirit grows faint within me, it is you who watch over my way." (NIV)

Ongoing Conversation

A third element of developing a life of prayer is maintaining an ongoing conversation with the Lord. This can happen while driving to work, before entering an important meeting, or before dozing off to sleep each night. It cultivates a relationship with God, remembering that He wants to have a "relationship" with you *not* a "religion" with you. You really can't have a relationship with somebody if you don't ever communicate.

I encourage you to talk to God throughout the day. But be careful that people don't think you are losing your mind! The other day I was taking a walk on the beach and talking to God. It was early in the morning. Not thinking anyone was watching me, I came up to the sidewalk, a car pulled up, the driver rolled down the window and said, "Talking to yourself? Don't let people think you're crazy." It was a member of my church, joking with me. I quipped back, "We all know I'm crazy! But I was just talking to God."

Take the risk and begin talking with the Lord every day. Committing to a life of prayer is not sweet and cute. It's powerful, adventurous, and dangerous!

Author Erwin McManus tells the story of one summer when his son Aaron went to a kid's camp. He was just a little guy, and so Erwin was glad that it was a church camp. He figured his boy wasn't going to hear all those ghost stories, because ghost stories can really cause a kid to have nightmares. But unfortunately, since it was a Christian camp and they didn't tell ghost stories (*because we don't believe in ghosts*), they told demon and Satan stories instead! So when Aaron got home, he was terrified. "Dad, don't turn off the light!" he said before going to bed. "No, Daddy, could you stay here with me? Daddy, I'm afraid. They told us these stories about demons." Erwin confesses he wanted to say, "They're not real," to ease his son. Aaron continued, "Daddy, Daddy would you pray for me that I would be safe?" Erwin said, "Aaron I will *not* pray for you to be safe. I will pray that God will make you dangerous, so dangerous that demons will flee when you enter the room." His son nervously agreed, "All right, Daddy. But pray I would be really, really dangerous!" I love the honesty of kids.

Committing to a life of prayer is not sweet and cute. It's powerful, adventurous, and dangerous!

Living a life of prayer makes you dangerous in a wonderful way. It places you in the thick of the grand scheme of things and the wonder of God's will. It makes life an adventure to be discovered. Once you know what God is calling you to do, it will require **The PERSONAL Factor**: walking out a life of purity, perseverance, purpose, and prayer. And there is nothing greater than walking those things out with absolute unadulterated passion! Take the final step in **The PERSONAL Factor**... passion.

Factor Five:
The PERSONAL Factor
Following God's Will for Your Life
Walking It Out: A Life of Passion

Chapter 25
A Life of Passion

"Consider him who endured such opposition from sinful men, so that you will not grow weary and lose heart."
Hebrews 12:3 (NIV)

Two of the challenges that can knock you off the path of completing God's will for your life are growing weary and losing heart. If you lose your passion for God, for life, for purpose, you will ultimately lose heart. And if you lose heart, you lose out on experiencing God's will. The weapon *against* growing weary is passion.

Passion Compels Us into Action

Passion simply means *intense love—compelling action.* Passion means loving God so intensely that it catapults you into action. Have you ever witnessed someone who catapults into action? It reminds me of my junior high Physical Education (PE) classes where "Coach" would have us wrestle. Most of us were scrawny 7th graders with oversized puffy gym shorts that needed to be grown into. The PE Coach would get two kids on the wrestling mat and shout, *"Wrastle!"* (Not "wrestle," rather, "wrastle.") One kid named Jerry was this unassuming quiet kid who was as scrawny as anyone. When Coach shouted, this junior high boy turned into a screaming super monster, running across the mat and tackling the other kid! He was the epitome of being catapulted into action. He had passion.

> The weapon *against* growing weary is passion.

One of the most passionate characters in the Bible is David in the Old Testament. He's described as a "man after God's own heart." Although he made some major life mistakes along the way, his passion for God burned fiery bright.

The Three Mighty Men

However, there are three guys in the Old Testament that had as much passion as David did, yet are rarely mentioned. The title for these three amigos is "the three mighty men." They were actually servants to their passionate leader, David. Here's the story: David and his soldiers are in an intense battle with the evil Philistines.

In 1 Chronicles 11:17 it says,

> "David longed for water and said, 'Oh, that someone would get me a drink of water from the well near the gate of Bethlehem!'" (NIV)

I love it. David sighs and throws out there, "Oh, that someone would get me a drink of water."

Well, these three mighty men hear David's wish and because of their intense love for David and the purposes of God, they were catapulted into action. They break through the enemy lines, draw water, and carry it back to David. Could you imagine fighting off attackers, doing a serpentine path through a battlefield while trying to balance and not spill a bucket of water?! If it wasn't for the fact that they were risking their lives, it's kind of a humorous picture. Yet, it was their passion that drove them to serve their leader and their God. David, being the passionate guy that he is, turns around and pours the water out onto the ground, not wanting to drink the water because the three mighty men risked their lives to get it.

Intense Love

Intense love compels everyday people into incredible action. I think of the pilgrims who were driven by a passion for freedom and a new life. They were so committed to what they believed was God's will they endured horrific conditions to get to their promised land. I heard a story where these settlers had to store their food in the bottom of the ship and eat the food in pitch dark because it had spoiled and was too grotesque to look at. How does anyone do that? Passion.

> Intense love compels everyday people
> into incredible action.

Passion takes an individual to a whole new level in life. And yet, it is easy to lose it.

As the writer of Hebrews says in 12:3,

> "Consider him who endured such opposition from sinful men, so that you will <u>not grow weary</u> and <u>lose heart</u>."
> (NIV; underlines added for emphasis)

When we think of the ultimate sacrifice that Jesus endured, it helps us continue the journey and complete God's will for our lives with passion.

Another definition of passion is illuminated in 2 Corinthians 5:14-15:

> "[14] For <u>Christ's love compels us</u>, because we are convinced that one died for all, and therefore all died. [15] And he died for all, that those <u>who live</u> should no longer live for themselves but <u>for him</u> who died for them and was <u>raised again</u>."
> (NIV; underlines added for emphasis)

When it says *Christ's love compels us* that is another way of saying *intense love—compelling action.* Part of God's will for your life means not living for yourself, which is selfish and self centered; rather, God's will for your life means living for the One who laid his life down for you, Jesus Christ. This reality is what brings meaning to life. Most people spend their lives in search of significance and meaning, yet feel empty. Even famous people who seem to have everything still feel the void in their soul.

The New England Patriots MVP quarterback, Tom Brady, is not only one of the NFL's best players; he is also one of the NFL's best stories. At the young age of 28, he had already won three Super Bowls, an accomplishment that ranks him with some of the best quarterbacks ever to play the game. Brady's loss to the Denver Broncos in the 2005 playoffs was his first in the playoffs, compared with ten playoff wins in the previous four years. But with all of Brady's fame and career accomplishments, he told *60 Minutes*: "Why do I have three Super Bowl rings and still think there's something greater out there for me? I mean, maybe a lot of people would say, 'Hey man, this is what it is. I reached my goal, my life.' Me, I think, 'God, it's got to be more than this.' I mean this isn't, this can't be, what it's all cracked up to be."

"What's the answer?" asked interviewer Steve Kroft. "I wish I knew," Brady replied. "I wish I knew."

The Hole in the Human Heart that Only Jesus Can Fill

There is a hole in the human heart and only Jesus can fill it. When a person invites Him to fill their heart, passion for life, God, and purpose arises. And that passion becomes the rocket fuel to launch you into the greatest journey of your life, knowing God's will.

God has a good, perfect, and pleasing will for your life. The ball is now in your court to discover, respond, and to pursue His will. That's **The PERSONAL Factor**: after discovering His will, to then walk it out.

If you will take the five factors and piece them together, you are going to experience the great joy of knowing God's will for your life. My encouragement is, "Go for it!"

Factor One: The YOU Factor—
Getting Ready
"...be transformed by the renewing of your mind..."
Romans 12:2

Factor Two: The GOD Factor—
Five Ways God Speaks to Us
"...God does speak..." **Job 33:14**

Factor Three: The GOD AND YOU Factor—
Receiving an Answer from God
"...what He will say to me..." Habakkuk 2:1

Factor Four: The TEST Factor—
Testing Your Decisions
"Test everything..." 1 Thessalonians 5:21

Factor Five: The PERSONAL Factor—
Following God's Will for Your Life
"...if you hear his voice, do not harden your hearts."
Hebrews 4:7

Where Do We Go from Here?

Discover God's Will — *Five Factors That Will Change Your Life Forever* created a journey that positioned you to hear from God. However, let's continue the journey. There are two more components that are absolutely vital for your success: God's purpose and God's peace.

So keep a lookout for two more books in our Discover God Series:

1. ***Discover God's Purpose*** — *Trusting Him Who Works All Things Together for Good*

2. ***Discover God's Peace*** — *In the Tough Times and All the Time*

Acknowledgements

First of all, thank you to my Mountainbrook Community Church Staff! You're the best. (Period)

To the family of Mountainbrook Community Church, thank you for your love and warmth for the last, oh say, 20 years! You've put up with my quirky sense of humor, have trusted my leadership, and have been gracious to me and my family. I'm overwhelmingly blessed to call you family.

I am thankful to my friend, Bob Kitamura, for his encouragement and support to "go for it" in life and on this book project. Bob, you have a unique gifting, like no other, which breeds wisdom, courage, and kindness all at the same time. When I grow up, I want to be like you!

There is an enormous amount of gratitude in my heart for Valerie Powell. Thank you for being the type of person with tenacious persistence. Your research behind the scenes made this book project possible. And it sure doesn't hurt that you are a prayer warrior!

Speaking of prayer warriors, words cannot accurately communicate my eternal gratefulness for Jerry Degarmo.

I call you my "Personal Prayer Warrior." You have weathered the storms and celebrated the victories with me over the last couple of decades. Where would I be without your endless intercession?

To Sue Hobler: thank you for the tedious editing! You have such a kind and gentle spirit. Thanks for being so willing to help me.

Brooke (O'Leary) Jeffrey, you made the final edits. You always have been great at details. "She shoots – she scores!" Thanks for making me better.

Sherri O'Leary, you have been my "personal" editor for over a quarter of a century! Thanks, babe.

David Pascolla your amazing photography is the bomb. Your friendship is equal!

Thanks to Stacy Pascolla for encouraging me to write, and for praying blessings upon me!

Josh George, your friendship is invaluable. Thanks for walking with me through the peaks and valleys of life. And since we both grew up in the valley—it makes sense.

To my new friend and publisher, Glen Aubrey and the people of Creative Team Publishing: you got me up and over the "publishing-mountain!" Glen, you have the gift of encouragement and your words are fuel to my soul.

A great big thanks to the Nelson clan. I married into a one-of-a-kind family for which I am forever grateful.

My heart is full of thanksgiving for my own family I grew up with. To the O'Leary-Beck clan... well, Mom and Dad (Ann and Joe)... it's your fault! You created some cool kids, who (who are we kidding?) all married up! I love you all.

Heart to Heart

We all have challenges and struggles, searching for God to intervene. I wrestle with this all the time. Not having all the answers, I desperately need His guidance and peace. I'm so grateful for God's Word that speaks so powerfully into our lives, giving us clear direction

Since becoming the Lead Pastor of Mountainbrook Community Church, in San Luis Obispo, CA, on the Central Coast, I continue to face major decisions all the time. I look back at when I started at age 28, and really didn't have much of a clue of what I was doing. I did have a lot of faith and trust in God. It's so true that church growth isn't manufactured; rather, it takes a listening ear to the promptings of God's Spirit.

I'm grateful to see His powerful work in the lives of "everyday people" like you and me, watching our church grow from 200 people to over 1,500 members. One of the biggest faith journeys I have traveled was leading the church into its first owned building that now sits on a spectacular 63 acres overlooking the city. That was a decade-long pursuit and a tremendous challenge—I can show you the scars to prove it! However, God is faithful.

The seasons of life will always change, and the demands will ebb and flow. I remember playing football at Cal Poly in the eighties, and now I serve as the Cal Poly Football Team Chaplain. Where does the time go?

Allowing God to use us in our community and context adds spice to life. Serving as the chairman on the San Luis Obispo Police Chief Round Table, creating a bridge of communication between the citizens and the police department, is one of the doors that God has opened for me. Another opportunity He has provided is serving as the Central California Regional Leader for Vineyard Churches— it's an honor and privilege to work with grace-filled, Spirit-driven, Kingdom-minded leaders who are committed and rooted in God's Holy Word.

I love communication. Whether ministering weekly through sermons, writing articles, emailing my weekly devotional "E-Heart to Heart" or radio broadcasting "Heart to Heart" and "Straight from the Heart" on both Christian and secular stations, I enjoy using communication to encourage, strengthen, and hopefully help transform human hearts. From my heart to yours, thank you for allowing me to communicate with you in *Discover God's Will—Five Factors That Will Change Your Life Forever.*

Life is short. Every heartbeat is a gift. May we discover God's will and give every fiber of our being to our last breath to fulfill it.

By His Grace,
Thom O'Leary

Products, Services, and Speaking Engagements

Thom O'Leary is available for speaking engagements for conferences, seminars, retreats, camps, and guest speaking. Please visit www.DiscoverGodSeries.com to contact him.

Other books coming in the Discover God Series:

1. *Discover God's Purpose* — Trusting Him Who Works All Things Together for Good
2. *Discover God's Peace* — In the Tough Times and All the Time

Sign up for Pastor Thom's weekly email devotional called "Heart to Heart" at www.DiscoverGodSeries.com.

www.DiscoverGodSeries.com

CPSIA information can be obtained at www.ICGtesting.com
Printed in the USA
BVOW080005080713

324941BV00003B/26/P